ELEANOR ROOSEVELT

A BIOGRAPHY

by
SALLY KNAPP

New York
THOMAS Y. CROWELL COMPANY

Copyright 1949 by Sally Knapp

All rights reserved. No part of this book may be reproduced in any form, except by a reviewer, without the permission of the publisher.

Designed by Maurice Serle Kaplan

Manufactured in the United States of America by Vail-Ballou Press, Inc., Binghamton, N. Y.

Printing Statement:

Due to the very old age and scarcity of this book, many of the pages may be hard to read due to the blurring of the original text, possible missing pages, missing text and other issues beyond our control.

Because this is such an important and rare work, we believe it is best to reproduce this book regardless of its original condition.

Thank you for your understanding.

CONTENTS

1. "LITTLE NELL" — 1
2. LIFE WITH GRANDMOTHER — 18
3. COMING OF AGE — 34
4. MARRIAGE AND A FAMILY — 52
5. "ELEANOR AND I" — 73
6. FIRST LADY — 88
7. MY DAY — 103
8. CHAMPION OF MINORITIES — 119
9. A THOUSAND AND ONE PROJECTS — 137
10. YOUNG PEOPLE — 150
11. THE LADY OF WASHINGTON SQUARE — 165
    INDEX — 183

1

"LITTLE NELL"

A SOLEMN-FACED little girl pressed her nose flat against the windowpane and stared anxiously out into the mid-town Manhattan street. She watched a sorrel horse, with proudly arched neck, go by. Sunlight reflected from his glistening coat and from the shiny black carriage with its smartly attired footmen sitting proudly up in front. Eleanor pressed her face even tighter against the window and twisted it unmercifully against the hard, cold glass, trying to see around the corner at the end of the row of brownstone houses. She strained her eyes to catch a first glimpse of a tall, dark-haired figure rounding the corner. But no one was in sight.

Sighing heavily, she turned back into the room. If she only knew what the mystery surrounding her father's absence was all about, this waiting wouldn't be so hard. Except for a few words she had overheard her mother whisper to her aunt about "Elliott's weakness," she knew only that her best friend had mysteriously gone away. He was returning today for a brief visit.

Reluctantly she settled down with a book into the massive, horsehair overstuffed chair. She had to sit way back, her feet pointing straight out, in order not to slip off. The hairs prickled her legs through their long white cotton stockings. The big white bow on Eleanor's hair drooped dejectedly. She blew her stubby bangs out of her eyes and pushed her shoulder-length bob back over her shoulders as she tried to read her book. It was two hours before her father was due to arrive, but he might come early. The words blurred on the page. She just couldn't concentrate on such a day.

Eleanor ran to the window and peered out ten times within the next half hour. Would he never come? She smoothed her white dress carefully and settled down again into the burnt-leather cushions and satin-faced pillows on the divan. She thumbed idly through the red plush photograph album she had already seen a dozen times. And then she glanced at the clock—a massive eight-day timepiece in the stomach of a plaster Venus de Milo.

"I'll play a game with myself. I won't look at the clock again until three people have passed the house." That took eight minutes. "I'll close my eyes and count from one to a hundred backwards before I look at the time again." That took six minutes.

At last it was four o'clock! Big, blue-gray eyes searched the street again. Around the corner came a sun-tanned, slim man, striding along with the peculiar gait of one who was more used to sitting astride a horse than walking city streets. His kind face was lighted with an expectation that matched her own. She ran out into the hall, pulled open the massive front door and was half way down the long flight of brownstone steps before he caught her in his arms. His bristly mustache tickled her cheek. "My little Nell!" He tossed her up in the air and held her suspended high above his head for a minute, while he peered into her face. Held close in his arms as they entered the house, Eleanor knew she had never been so happy.

Joyous occasions such as this had been very few in recent years for Eleanor. With her father away so much of the time, she didn't have even his companionship to offset her mother's obvious disapproval of her. She tried hard, but she could not live up to her mother's impossible standards. Anna Roosevelt tried, too, but she could not understand a daughter who was not quite like everyone else. Tradition and environment were too strongly entrenched in her.

Anna Hall Roosevelt was descended from a signer of the Declaration of Independence. All the Hall girls were noted for their beauty and charm in the exclusive Society of the eighties, which took such matters as beauty and family aristocracy very seriously. Society—always spelled with a capital "S"—considered itself all-important in those days. Certain things "were done." Anything else was in bad taste, if not downright wicked. Society invited only the right people to its homes and accepted invitations only from these same people.

Society had its charities, of course. It helped hospitals and other institutions for the poor, doing all the correct kindnesses for the unfortunate. But Society scorned to mingle with the poor; all contacts were by remote control. There was nothing here of personal interest and self-sacrificing kindness.

Eleanor's mother had gone to the accepted fashionable schools and read only what everyone else read. Because Grandfather Hall had been strict and set in his ways, Anna Roosevelt's ideas of right and wrong conformed to a rigid conventional pattern. Everything was black or white; there were no intermediate softening shades of gray. She never questioned a command or wondered whether a statement was true. And she never thought to ask "why."

There was a way of life Grandfather Hall had prescribed as the "proper existence for a lady." It was quite typical of his child-raising methods, for instance, to insist that Anna and her sister Tissie walk from the house on their country estate to the main road several times a day with a stick across their backs in the crook of their elbows, to improve their posture and carriage. Such discipline may have "strengthened Anna's character"—at least it made her more rigid—but unfortunately it never gave her a chance to develop any tolerance for the weaknesses and temptations of others.

When Anna Hall was seventeen, her father died and she, as the eldest child, became head of the house. At nineteen she married Elliot Roosevelt.

Eleanor's father, Elliott, was Theodore Roosevelt's brother. Born into the same society as his wife, he had found illness an escape from its severe pattern. At fifteen he had been sent to Texas to hunt and scout for Indians with the army officers at a frontier post. He regained his health, became an enthusiastic horseman, and took a trip around the world before he returned to New York to marry and settle down in Manhattan society. He was not so interested in its social whirl as was his wife, but he took part in it readily enough, especially its sports. He played polo on Long Island, and occasionally went off, with his fellow sportsmen, on hunting trips to India and the West. He took a more personal interest in people than his wife did, and he spent considerable time carrying on the work his father had started, with the newsboys and crippled children of New York.

Eleanor was a very welcome first child to these two, devoted to each other despite the fact that they didn't see many things eye to eye. To her father, Eleanor was a miracle from heaven, his chief joy in life. As soon as she was old enough to toddle, she became his daily companion in everything he did. Summers spent at their summer home in Hempstead, Long Island, with the horses and dogs that both Eleanor and her father loved, were particularly happy times.

As she grew older, Eleanor realized that only in her lack of physical courage was she a disappointment to her father. Her fears stemmed naturally from several harrowing childhood experiences. One night, while she was bound for Europe with her family, the boat Eleanor was on was run down by another steamer during a fog. Her father stood in a lifeboat below, and the terrified little girl was dangled over the side and dropped into his arms. Shrieking wildly, she clung to those who were dropping her. Her family set sail again on another ship—but without Eleanor. She would not go near the boat and had to be left at home. Her fear of the water stayed with her for many years.

Her natural timidity was increased by another experience. She was riding with her maid in a dismal, horse-drawn streetcar, through the Manhattan streets. Smelly oil lamps dimly lit the interior. As the car stopped to let passengers off, a wretched looking man jumped in and snatched a purse from the woman sitting next to Eleanor. Everyone screamed and yelled, "Stop thief!" Eleanor, in a panic, shot out of the streetcar, into the midst of the milling crowd. Like a small, frightened animal, she pushed her way through the horde of people, turning first this way, then that, not knowing where to go. She was finally rescued and brought home, but the face of the "poor man" continued to haunt her dreams for months, in a mixture of confusion and noise.

Eleanor tried hard to conquer her fears—she

wanted, more than anything else, to please her father —but after these early mishaps it was a long, uphill struggle for a shy little girl. However, Eleanor never doubted that she stood first in her father's heart. "My earliest recollections are of being dressed up and allowed to come down to the dining room and dance for a group of gentlemen, who laughed as I pirouetted before them. Then my father would pick me up and hold me high in the air. He dominated my life as long as he lived, and was the love of my life for many years after he died."

Before long, a black cloud descended on this happy family. The strain of increased social and business activities was too much for Elliott Roosevelt's uncertain health. His physical weakness as a boy had left its mark. When an emergency calling for great fortitude arose, his inner reserve of strength was not there. A long, painful ordeal with a broken leg, which had to be broken and reset several times, tipped the scales. His balance was lost, never to be completely regained. He began to drink heavily.

After Eleanor's brother, Elliott Jr., was born, the family went abroad to Italy and France, in a desperate attempt to help Elliott Sr. regain his health and self-control. First he went to a sanatorium, and Eleanor, with her mother and small brother, settled down in a bungalow in Neuilly, outside Paris. It was both a happy and an unhappy trip for Eleanor. She knew that something was wrong with her father, though no one thought it wise to explain it to her. She suffered silently over the mystery, much more miserable over this uncertainty than she would ever have been over the truth.

"If people only realized what a war goes on in a child's mind and heart in a situation of this kind, I think they would try to explain to children more than they do," she said later.

But there were happy times, too. On her father's good days, Eleanor accompanied him on sightseeing tours around Paris. Later she went on Venetian canalboat trips, with her father acting as gondolier, or on hikes over the rugged countryside of northern Italy. Climbing up and down the steep, rocky hills was quite a terrifying experience for a five-and-a-half-year-old, but Eleanor tried never to let her father know she was afraid.

Many of the traits that later became an integral part of Eleanor Roosevelt's character show in incidents of her childhood. Trivial in themselves, they nevertheless foretold something of the woman she was to become.

One day the two travelers stopped at Sorrento, in Italy. Eleanor was fascinated by the donkey boy and his sturdy animals. "Come," her father said, seeing her interest. "Take a ride over the hills. The boy will run alongside and guide the donkey. The roads through the hills are so beautiful right now." He motioned down the winding dirt road, in the direction of emerald fields and azure skies. "I'll sit here and wait until you return."

Eleanor mounted the small, chunky animal willingly enough, and her father watched the two start down the long road, the little donkey boy running alongside, his bare feet skillfully picking the way past rocks and trees, his straw hat flopping around his ears. Eleanor looked back over her shoulder and waved to her father, just as the road, dipping below the horizon, took her out of sight.

Elliott Roosevelt sat up suddenly and rubbed his eyes. He looked at his watch. Surely they wouldn't be coming back so soon! But there were three figures unmistakably headed toward him. He looked again, jumped up, and ran out to meet them. "What's wrong?" he asked his daughter who, panting and perspiring, was running alongside the donkey, while the boy, grinning happily, sat astride the placid animal.

"Nothing, Father—really—" Eleanor answered. "His feet were cut and bleeding, and I felt so sorry for him I couldn't enjoy the ride. It's better this way, 'cause I have shoes." She smiled at him, and he snatched her up in his arms.

Another time, in a German cafe, Eleanor sat with her father watching the children drink a delicious-looking amber liquid. He told her several times that she would not like it. After she had begged very hard, however, her father consented to let her have a mug of beer, but warned her, "Remember, if you take it, you'll have to drink the whole mugful." Eleanor took a sip and nearly choked. She made a wry face. She had expected something sweet and delicious—like honey. That's what it looked like. But she took a deep breath and drank the bitter draft to the last drop.

Perhaps Eleanor's teetotalism in her adult life was due as much to this distasteful incident as to her more serious experiences with alcohol and its effects. Anyway, she never drank beer again.

Eleanor's European travels ended abruptly. Her

father returned to the sanatorium, and the little girl was placed in a French convent, to be conveniently absent while a third child was born. She was very unhappy there. Her playmates spoke a strange language, and their interests were quite different from hers. She walked alone through the gardens of the convent, hemmed in by stone walls which kept her from her father. She was hungry for the attention and friendship of others, but had no idea how to get it. Conscious of her plain looks and lack of manners, she deeply desired affection and praise.

One day at the convent, a little French girl who accidently swallowed a penny was the center of excited interest for several hours. It seemed a good way to get attention, so Eleanor succumbed to temptation and pretended to swallow one. The Sister didn't believe her and, when Eleanor insisted, sent for her mother. Eleanor went back to the cottage in disgrace. Her mother was outraged: "How could any daughter of mine be such a liar!" She didn't realize that it was only a lonely child's effort to gain attention.

"My mother didn't understand that a child may lie from fear, too. I could bear swift punishment of any kind far better than long scoldings. I would cheerfully lie any time to escape a scolding. But if I knew I would simply be put to bed or spanked, I usually told the truth."

After the baby, Hall, was born, Anna Roosevelt and her three children sailed for home, leaving their father in the sanatorium in France. Eleanor never saw her father after that except for short visits because, though he returned to the United States, he became a recluse in the West Virginia mountains.

Eleanor was nearly seven when the family returned to Manhattan and her mother decided that her formal education should begin. They moved to a smaller house on East 61st Street, and Mrs. Roosevelt organized a class, of her friends' and her own children, to meet there daily. A fashionable teacher was engaged to instruct the group in reading, writing, sewing, French, and other suitable subjects.

Anna Roosevelt reserved time every afternoon for her children. She took an interest in all their activities and made a special effort with her daughter. But Eleanor always felt like an outsider, somehow different and apart from her brothers. They seemed so close to their mother, and she missed her father so much. "Mother was troubled by my lack of beauty, and tried very hard to bring me up well so that my manners would in some way compensate for my looks, but her efforts only made me more keenly conscious of my shortcomings."

Mrs. Roosevelt made a great effort to understand her daughter, but for some reason the barrier was always there. Unconsciously she always did things that accentuated the girl's shyness. Looking up as Eleanor entered the room where her mother was entertaining a visitor, she would say, "Come in, Granny." And to the visitor she would add, "She's such a funny child, so old-fashioned." At such times, in an agony of self-consciousness, Eleanor wished she could sink through the floor.

When she could be useful, Eleanor's loneliness seemed to ebb for awhile. Her mother had rather frequent, excrutiating headaches, and Eleanor's greatest joy was to sit at the head of the bed and stroke her mother's soft, shiny hair, erasing with her smooth touch the strain of a bitter life. Often the little girl kept at it for hours, until both her arms ached.

Although they did not understand each other very well, Eleanor admired her mother greatly. "She was one of the most beautiful women I have ever seen," she said. Eleanor's chief delight was watching her mother dress for a party. She could do this often, because, as was the custom then, they shared a room.

"LITTLE NELL"

Eleanor loved her mother, but seemed doomed always to disgrace her. In her small class, when she was asked to spell some simple words, Eleanor was a complete failure. "What is the matter with you? You know those words perfectly well," her mother would say, exasperatedly. And it was true. Eleanor knew the words, but she was too shy to open her mouth.

One of the greatest bones of contention between Eleanor and her mother was Eleanor's love for sweets and sugar, which had been forbidden by the family doctor. Her sweet tooth often led her into the pantry when she knew dinner-party candy would be abundant. She would eat on the spot all she could cram into her mouth. Sometimes she even risked putting some in a paper bag and hiding it down the front of her dress. The crackling usually gave her away before she could make the safety of her room, and she'd be sent to bed in disgrace.

A second scheme worked a little better, for a time. Sugar on cereal was not allowed, but since Eleanor ate breakfast by herself from a tray in the library, it was often possible to coax one of the servants to bring her some sugar. One morning her mother walked into the room just as she was covering her cereal heavily with sugar. She was caught at last!

In spite of such minor irritations, life on the whole went smoothly and pleasantly in the Roosevelt home for a year after their return from Europe. Then this ordered existence suddenly changed. Eleanor's mother died of diphtheria. Death itself meant nothing to the little girl. She hardly realized it was a time of sorrow. She only knew that something had happened which was going to bring her father home. Her joy because of that overshadowed everything else.

Elliott Roosevelt arrived from West Virginia too late to see his wife before she died. This was hard enough, but his heart was broken when he discovered that she had designated her mother as guardian for his three children. Not that he blamed her for feeling he couldn't be trusted with their care, but it cut deeply. As Eleanor said, "He had no hope now of ever wiping out the sorrowful years he had brought upon my mother. He had no wife, no children, no hope!"

The grief-stricken man talked and planned with his "Little Nell" the home they would have some day, the places they would see together, the things they would do together. She promised to study hard, and to make a special effort to excel at music, although she had no ability for it.

Elliott Roosevelt went back to West Virginia, and

"LITTLE NELL"

Eleanor was left to live in a dream world, in which she talked constantly with her father and planned the many wonderful things they would do together. She was left alone, to keep their secret of mutual understanding and to adjust herself to a new existence.

2

LIFE WITH GRANDMOTHER

ELEANOR and her two young brothers went to to live with Grandmother Hall. Also living in the somber house were two young aunts and two young uncles, who "never by word or deed made any of us feel that we were not in our own house." Elliott Jr. died of diphtheria, and Eleanor and her baby brother, Hall, were left to bring a little laughter and childish noise into the big, gloomy house.

It was a fashionable home on 37th Street in Manhattan. There were many large rooms with high ceilings, furnished in a rather formal way. The dark basement, with its cramped servant quarters and tiny, ill-ventilated rooms—"working conditions no one with any social conscience would tolerate today"— bothered Eleanor. So did all the misery she saw on the streets of New York. Her governess or one of the French maids took her safely through those streets every day, past a number of large and beautiful homes on Fifth Avenue, down Madison Avenue, which was still almost entirely residential, down to 23rd Street, where the shopping district began.

Grandmother Hall soon allowed Eleanor to begin philanthropic work, but only the kind considered suitable for a member of the "aristocracy." She went to the Orthopaedic Hospital to visit the crippled children of the poor. This project had always been her father's particular interest, and his father's before him.

Eleanor stopped to talk with a red-headed boy encased in a steel brace from shoulders to hips. "It's a nuisance, isn't it?" she said sympathetically. "See—I have one too." She took off her coat to show him. Eleanor had been put in a temporary brace to help improve her posture.

The little boy's eyes lighted. "I hate not being able to bend over—don't you?" he said. She agreed and they went on talking together like old friends.

Thanks to her Uncle Vallie, though, Eleanor learned more about the life of the poor than this family philanthropy would ever have taught her. He took her with him to help trim a Christmas tree for the children in "Hell's Kitchen," one of New York's worst slums. Eleanor always suspected that her very popular, society-minded uncle was not interested solely in charitable work when he made these frequent visits. She felt that his zeal had something to do with a charming young lady of his acquaintance, who was interested in these same "good works."

Whatever her other activities, a daily walk in the park was regular routine, weather permitting. Eleanor would walk fast and furiously, with the maid trying desperately to keep up with her. Eleanor didn't want to talk to anyone. She preferred to be left alone in her dream world, "where I was the heroine and my father the hero." Her father influenced her life in many small ways. For instance, she had a habit of biting her nails until, in one of her father's letters, she came across a paragraph in which he emphasized the importance of good personal appearance. From then on her nails were allowed to grow.

Eleanor always believed that she and her father would some day have a life of their own together. Elliott Roosevelt's visits to his children were very irregular. He seldom sent word beforehand, but Eleanor, hearing his voice the moment he stepped in the door, would come sliding down the banister from her room, and land in his arms before he even had a chance to hang up his hat and coat.

She was not quite ten when the center of Eleanor's universe dropped out. Her father died. Despite the previous loss of her mother, she had had no real experience with death, having been carefully shielded from it by her grandmother. At first she refused to believe her father was dead. "Although each night I went to bed weeping, I finally went to sleep. And awoke the next morning to begin living in my dream world again."

Unfortunately Eleanor's well-meaning but not very understanding grandmother decided the children should not go to the funeral, so Eleanor had nothing tangible to make death real to her. "I knew in my mind that my father was dead, but my heart refused to accept it. I lived with him more closely, probably, than I had when he was alive." It took quite a while for Eleanor to realize finally that she was not going to see her father again in this world. Even so, he remained an important influence in her life for many years.

Grandmother Hall saw to it that practically all contact with the Roosevelt family was cut off. "Perhaps she feared that we would slip from her control if we were too much with our dynamic Roosevelt relations." Grandmother had long since lost control over her own children and she was determined that her grandchildren should have the discipline her sons and daughters lacked.

"We were brought up on the principle that 'no' was easier to say than 'yes.' And it was not necessary to give a reason for a refusal either—just enough that Grandmother thought it unwise."

Grandmother Hall said "No" so consistently that Eleanor often pretended not to want to do things she really wanted to do very much, to avoid disappointment.

Although still quite young, Grandmother Hall kept almost entirely to her bedroom. She came downstairs only to entertain occasional visitors of her own in the parlor. Nevertheless she prescribed from her Ivory Tower every little detail of Eleanor's studies, her clothes, and even her bathing. Two hot baths a week and a cold sponge every morning was the rule, but Eleanor cheated a little on these cold baths in winter.

Grandmother wished to keep Eleanor as young in dress as possible. So although her granddaughter was a thin, gangly girl, a good deal taller than other girls her age, she forced her to wear, at parties and dancing classes, clothes perhaps appropriate to her age, but not to her size. Eleanor's clothes were usually made over from someone else's, and she quickly grew out of them. Her dresses were above her knees when other girls her size wore their skirts half way down their legs. She was tortured by being different.

High laced shoes, supposed to keep ankles slim, emphasized her legginess. From November to April, no matter what the weather, she had to wear flannel from her neck to her ankles, bulky petticoats, and long black stockings. Even in summer these stockings had to be worn. This was a hangover from Grandmother's youth, when children were wrapped in heavy flannel petticoats, padded dresses, and padded hats, so that a child couldn't hurt herself if she fell. Of course, she could hardly move or breathe, either.

On breathlessly hot summer days, her fingers stuck to the keys as she practiced the piano. But if Eleanor dared roll her stockings down, she was told by her grandmother that ladies did not show their legs, and the horrid black stockings had to be fastened up again.

The children's education, too, was dictated by Grandmother, who had peculiar tastes in such matters. They learned verse after verse of the New Testament in French! "I thought it a great waste of time then, but later found very useful the trained memory which all this learning of things by heart gave me," Eleanor admits. "If only we have been taught to reason, too."

Eleanor usually obeyed most of these many regulations without protest. Only on one score did she deliberately defy orders. She insisted upon secretly reading in bed before breakfast. She hid the book under the mattress and woke up at five each morning to get in an hour or two of reading before the maid came to call her. She read just about everything in her grandfather's huge library, including a Bible with fiery illustrations by Doré, which fascinated her but also gave her nightmares.

"No one tried to censor my reading, but when I happened on a book I couldn't understand and asked too many difficult questions before guests, the book would mysteriously disappear. I remember spending days hunting for one book and wondering where I could have left it." No book was forbidden her, though, and since then she has never felt it did her any harm to have this freedom in her choice of reading.

Summers at Oak Terrace, Tivoli, were considerably freer and pleasanter than life in Manhattan. On this Hudson River estate of her grandfather's, only Sunday was strictly regulated. No games were permitted then, of course; only religious songs could be sung; and only "Sunday" books could be read. These books were not read on other days, but were set aside especially for the Sabbath. There was pleasant Sunday evening hymn singing, with Aunt Pussie playing the piano in the parlor.

The whole family drove four miles to church every Sunday in the huge victoria coach. And little Eleanor, in true lady-of-the-manor style, was required, on her return home, to teach Bible verses, hymns, and catechism to the coachman's daughter every Sunday afternoon.

"A cold supper was still served Sunday evenings, although we didn't live up to the cold meal in the middle of the day, which had been Grandfather's rule," Eleanor remembers.

During the week Eleanor's days were full of a variety of activities. Piano practice was daily routine. There never was a child who had less talent for music, but the piano lessons continued. "I worked at music until I was eighteen, but no one could ever train my ear," she once remarked wryly. But she did gain an emotional appreciation of music, not only from this familiarity with many musical selections but also from listening to her Aunt Pussie, who was a gifted pianist.

Her Aunts Pussie and Maude, and Uncles Vallie and Eddie played games with her and occasionally took her riding or camping in the woods and cooked supper over a campfire. But Eleanor's best friend during these summers at Tivoli was the washerwoman, Mrs. Overholse, a cheerful, friendly person who came every day to wash and iron the huge family laundry, besides directing her own farm and rearing a considerable number of children. Eleanor loved to wash and iron but enjoyed most of all the happy company of this energetic, jolly woman. Sometimes Mrs. Overholse would invite Eleanor to spend a day on her farm and feed her good German cooking.

Eleanor was on good terms with all the servants. Often, when she was sent supperless to bed in disgrace, Victor the butler, or Kitty the chambermaid, would smuggle something for her to eat.

The rest of her free time was spent in a little house built in the woods for her at her grandmother's order. She spent many happy hours there, cooking, playing, reading, dreaming alone—for she had almost no companions. The nearest girl of Eleanor's age lived five miles away. She felt this lack keenly, especially later on, when she realized that having so few companions of her own age put her at a great disadvantage with other young people.

Her only other companions were the dogs and horses on the large estate. Eleanor always had a dog of her own, given to her by an aunt or uncle, or one of their friends. One of her many dogs was a white polar bear puppy of no recognizable breed, named Mickey. He was very intelligent, could even follow a hansom through crowded New York traffic.

Eleanor's favorite story about him was the trip he took from Hyde Park to New York. "We left him in the country and took a train to Grand Central Station. Evidently he followed us and took a later train going in the same direction, because the next morning he was on our doorstep. Later that day we got a call from one of the conductors on the train. 'Your dog got into the baggage car at Hyde Park, rode down by himself and got out at Grand Central,' he said. 'I just wanted to make sure he got home safely.'"

Another of Eleanor's pets was a pony, given to her by her father. She was not very happy in the saddle. She was so timid that the pony usually took her for a ride any place that suited him. She never felt at any time that she was "riding" him. But she felt better when he was hitched to a little cart and she and Hall and the nurse went driving along the country roads around Tivoli. She became not only familiar with the countryside, but very friendly with the farm people living in that section.

Eleanor's greatest trial at this time was sewing. "I hemmed endless dish towels and darned numberless stockings. And if a darn didn't suit my very particular governess, that heartless person took a pair of scissors and simply cut the whole thing out, leaving a much larger hole to be filled in all over again. I shed many a tear over this."

The house at Tivoli was very large, having nine master bedrooms on the second and third floors, and four double and one single servants' rooms. There were just two bathrooms in this huge mansion. High ceilings added still more space, especially to an expansive formal parlor, which had the usual marble mantelpieces, and chandeliers for candles. Beautiful china and silver and enameled pieces collected by members of the family from various parts of the world stood on mantelpieces and shelves.

In the basement was a large storeroom to which Eleanor followed her grandmother every morning. There they measured and weighed out the supplies of flour, sugar, and coffee for the day. Then Eleanor carried them up to the cook, who worked in a semidark kitchen. This kitchen was overshadowed by the piazza which extended half way around the house, and there was no gas or electricity, at that time, for her to work by.

Grandmother Hall thought dancing lessons—particularly ballet—would help overcome Eleanor's awkwardness. Eleanor enjoyed dancing but never acquired the grace her grandmother hoped for. Her only contact with boys her own age was at the annual Christmas Party at her Uncle Ted's home in Oyster Bay. This visit of a few days was a high spot in the year, representing a rare opportunity to be away from home overnight. "My young aunts had not been allowed, until they were seventeen, to stay overnight with anyone. In those days, guarding a girl was considered so difficult that I think my grandmother often prayed over it."

However, these parties were more pain than pleasure to Eleanor because of her extreme shyness. It is hard to believe that a woman who became one of the world's most gracious hostesses could ever have been such a wallflower. She was not too good a dancer, and the inappropriate dresses above her knees, which her grandmother still insisted she wear, made her self-conscious. Her unfamiliarity with boy-girl associations certainly did not help her to be at ease at a party.

At one such party she was sitting quietly, on a chair at one side of the dance floor, when a tall, handsome boy came over and asked her for a dance. Perhaps his kind heart had been attracted by the look of torment in her eyes.

Franklin immediately liked his solemn cousin with the large blue-gray eyes and long amber hair. The radiant pleasure in her face as she stepped out onto the dance floor with him, made her beautiful for that moment—as happiness often makes lovely the plainest of faces. He liked the way a smile lit up her entire face and the original way she had of thinking. He enjoyed talking with her. "She has a very good mind," he told his mother the morning after the dance.

Besides the dances, there were many strenuous sports at Uncle Ted's. Eleanor was expected to ice skate with the group, but she didn't know how to skate and was too afraid of the water, even though it was frozen, to learn. Her fears kept her out of many activities in her "growing-up years."

Only one thing could conquer Eleanor's timidity and fear of a dozen nameless things—an opportunity to be useful to someone she cared for. She was afraid of the dark, and of burglars, because one had once entered her grandmother's room and taken her rings. She could conquer her fear completely, however, when Aunt Pussie needed an ice pack for her headache. One night Eleanor stole down three flights of stairs to the pitch-black basement and on out to the icebox in the back yard. Her fear of going was not as great as her fear of not being allowed to administer to her fascinating and lovely aunt.

Back for the winters in Manhattan, Eleanor continued her studies and social activities. She was allowed to see some of Shakespeare's plays and, occasionally, the opera, but her grandmother didn't want her to attend any of the popular plays of the day. Her young aunts saw many plays, and discussed them with such enthusiasm that Eleanor was consumed with curiosity to see just one—any one.

At last this urge got the better of her. "Janet," she said one day to a friend her own age who lived on the next block, "we've just got to see a play. 'Tess of the D'Urbervilles' is playing now at the Orpheum. Maybe, if we pretended we were going to the charity bazaar . . ."

"But Eleanor," her friend objected, "you know your grandmother won't let you go even to a bazaar without your maid along."

"I think I can get rid of Ann." Blue eyes shone bright with mischief. "I'll let her think your maid is going with us."

Two excited girls, dressed in their best, made their way fearfully, with many backward glances, to the theater. They climbed carefully up to the last section in the balcony and settled down into their seats. Eleanor slid down in the seat until her head was below the top of the back rest. "Do you think there's anyone here who knows us?" she whispered to Janet.

"I hope not," came the hoarse reply.

Another long silence, while the two girls concentrated their attention on the stage for a few minutes. Then Eleanor whispered again, "Do you understand what this is all about?"

"Well, no," Janet admitted, shifting in her seat. A little later she said, "Guess we'd better go now or we'll get home too late."

LIFE WITH GRANDMOTHER

Eleanor protested feebly that the play wasn't over yet, but there was wisdom in what Janet had said. So they crept out of the theater and ran a good part of the way home, stopping only once to swear each other to eternal secrecy.

"Did you have a good time at the bazaar, dear?" Grandmother Hall asked Eleanor that evening.

"Y-yes," Eleanor stammered, and hurried out of the room. The shameful deed was never discovered by Grandmother, but it weighed so heavily on Eleanor's oversensitive conscience that she would gladly have confessed to be rid of the load. However, that would have involved Janet—so she suffered silently.

Suddenly Eleanor's life was changed again. Grandmother Hall decided that her household now had too much gaiety for a girl of fifteen, and that an education in Europe was in order.

3
―――

COMING OF AGE

THE following fall, Eleanor set sail for England with her Aunt Tissie. They had hardly climbed the gangplank to board the ship when Aunt Tissie turned to Eleanor and said dolefully, "I'm a very poor sailor, I'm going below now and go to bed. I won't be out of the cabin again until we reach England."

Eleanor was rather disappointed. This didn't sound like an interesting way to cross the ocean. But trained to obedience, and unschooled in the way of ocean voyages, Eleanor took her cue from Aunt Tissie. Thinking it the usual procedure she retired to her cabin for the rest of the voyage. Not only did she get very little pleasure out of her trip lying in a berth, but she also arrived in England quite wobbly in the knees, from her long period of inactivity.

Eleanor was enrolled in a school called Allenswood, not far from London. London seemed a tremendous city, even to a New Yorker. "I would go for hours in any direction and apparently still be in the center of the great city." Mlle. Souvestre, head of Allenswood, had educated Eleanor's Auntie Bye—her father's sister—and this personal tie made Grandmother Hall feel that her ward would be properly supervised and educated in this school.

The regime was quite strict, but Eleanor thoroughly enjoyed her three years at Allenswood. The first rule was that everyone had to speak French, and if a student used an English word she had to report herself at the end of the day. Since Eleanor had spoken French before she could speak English, thanks to a French nurse, this was not a difficult rule for her to obey. A little more difficult was the rule that each bath must be limited to ten minutes, and Eleanor found that she had to fight for more than two baths in a week.

Allenswood students had to make their own beds before leaving their rooms in the morning. Often, during the daily inspection, beds were stripped and left to be made over again. Even bureau drawers and closets had to be in perfect order. If they weren't, a girl might return to her room to find the entire contents of one or more drawers dumped in a pile in the middle of the bed.

Mlle. Souvestre was short and rather stout, with snow-white hair. She had a beautiful, strong face, with clear-cut features and a broad forehead. "She had an eagle eye which penetrated right through to your backbone and she took in everything about you," was Eleanor's comment.

Although Mlle. Souvestre did not believe in the righteousness of the English cause in the Boer War, which was now raging, and never took any pains to hide her feeling, she was fair. She did not expect the British girls to feel as she did. English victories were celebrated and holidays were allowed, but Mlle. Souvestre never took part in any of them. She was, to Eleanor, a fine example of tolerance for the different beliefs of others.

Eleanor learned many useful lessons from Mlle. Souvestre. She learned to love history because Mlle. Souvestre taught it so vividly and interestingly. Sitting opposite her, in the seat of honor, Eleanor acquired eating habits that she has "never been quite able to shake off." Mlle. Souvestre insisted that you need not take on your plate any more than you wanted, but you had to eat all you took. She also insisted that her students try a little of everything—even when they were being served a cold, clammy suet pudding. In spite of this, Eleanor always enjoyed her meals at Mlle. Souvestre's table.

Often there were interesting guests, and Eleanor enjoyed "eavesdropping" on their conversations. Her quick mind would store up new ideas and pieces of information for future conversations with Mlle. Souvestre. Since Mlle. Souvestre did most of the talking at these sessions, Eleanor never had to show her superficial knowledge of the subject, and of course Mlle. Souvestre was pleased at her interest.

Eleanor lived to regret this bad habit of "picking" other people's minds. She discovered she couldn't use the knowledge, which others had worked hard to acquire, for very long without stumbling over her own inadequacy. She learned that it took study and hard work to learn thoroughly any subject. Nevertheless, these experiences with Mlle. Souvestre and her guests resulted in a "speaking acquaintance" with many topics, which added immeasurably to her interests as she went through life.

Mlle. Souvestre heartily disapproved of Eleanor's clothes. "Frankly, I advise a few changes," she said in her meticulous French. "I recommend that you have a new dress." Many of Eleanor's dresses were made over from Maude's and Pussie's, and Mlle. Souvestre thought it was time she had at least one dress of her own, made to order. Although her family was quite wealthy, Eleanor's allowance was pitifully small. She rarely had an extra dime, because Grandmother Hall, who had seen her own sons and daughters squander their inheritances, kept a tight hold on her granddaughter's purse strings. She never let Eleanor know that she would eventually inherit a considerable sum of money. So Eleanor had to use part of her holiday allowance to get this new dress—a beautiful dark red one, reserved for special occasions.

When she first arrived at Allenswood, Eleanor shed some of the flannel underclothing her grandmother had always insisted that she wear, but before long she was back in it again, needing such protection against the damp cold of England. The students at Allenswood crowded into the dining room to get a seat as near the radiator as possible. In spite of the fact that during her three-year stay she was seldom warm, except in midsummer, Eleanor never felt better in her life. She wasn't ill a day.

Other vistas were opened up to Eleanor at Allenswood. She became an excellent hockey player—the

COMING OF AGE

first sport at which she had ever excelled. "At first I was as awkward as ever at games. I had never even seen a game of hockey, but I had to play something. In time I made the first team. That day was one of the proudest of my life." Some sport such as tennis, which she could have continued later in her life, would have been more useful, but Eleanor enjoyed this opportunity to play with others on a team. It was a completely new experience for her.

Eleanor's musical education continued. She practiced three hours a day, hours which might have been more profitably used elsewhere, since she rarely touched the piano in her later life. "I may have gained something in character, however, from getting up on dreary mornings and going into a cold room to practice on the piano before breakfast," she once said ruefully.

Eleanor had never had to take any personal responsibility for her actions. Her grandmother had prescribed her daily routine. She had never had to plan an activity in detail, as there were always servants to supervise such matters. But, now, while traveling with Mlle. Souvestre on summer holidays, she had responsibility thrust at her.

The wise old lady placed most of the responsibilities

of the trip on Eleanor's sixteen-year-old shoulders. She felt that this was the only way to make a young person self-reliant. Eleanor packed and unpacked for both of them, looked up trains, purchased the tickets, and arranged all details.

"I am an old lady, not up to endless hours of sightseeing, but you must see things for yourself," Mlle. Souvestre would say, as she sent Eleanor out alone into a strange city—a procedure which would have horrified Grandmother Hall had she known. Although Eleanor got lost now and then, she found people helpful and kind, and she gained in independence. "I felt I was starting a new life—free from all former traditions and restrictions."

They went to Paris, Switzerland and Italy, France, Belgium, and Germany. Mlle. Souvestre knew how to get the most out of traveling and how to enjoy it. "She always ate native dishes and drank native wines. I think she felt that it was just as important to enjoy good Italian food as it was to enjoy Italian art, and it all served to make you a citizen of the world, at home wherever you might go," Eleanor said admiringly.

At Grandmother Hall's request, Eleanor returned home for the summer vacation between her second and third years at Allenswood. It was a terrible ordeal.

COMING OF AGE

Eleanor couldn't get back to England soon enough!

She had nothing in common with the young people in her social set. She was completely wrapped up in her European school life and her many friends there. These young people at home were strangers to her. Because their interests were so different from hers, she found them hard to understand. She felt the anxiety of her relatives on every side, and shrank from it. They were worried because there seemed little hope that she would ever have any beaus.

Eleanor would have liked to stay a fourth year at Allenswood. Just the thought of leaving Mlle. Souvestre brought tears to her eyes, and she certainly had little reason to look forward to her return home. But according to Grandmother Hall, eighteen was the age to "come out," and not to "come out" was unthinkable. Soon after her arrival home, Eleanor tentatively suggested that she would like to go to college. But her grandmother was horrified. In her social circle, girls who made such suggestions were "not quite bright." So Eleanor resigned herself to her first season in New York society.

Eleanor had gained a great deal from her three years in Europe. She had learned how to live with others her own age. She had gained self-confidence and was more at ease in the company of others. She had further developed her strong sense of duty and obligation; but now she was learning to turn it into less rigid channels—to use it as a means of helping others. Her total education had been a strange mixture of extreme restriction and unlimited freedom. Though she had a strong desire to help others, yet she was unprepared in many ways even to take care of herself. She remained innocent and naive in spite of experience which should have made her sophisticated.

Years in Europe had given Eleanor her first taste of being carefree and irresponsible, but this feeling didn't last long. Several problems confronted her on returning home to New York. Uncle Vallie, who had always seemed steady, although romantic, began to drink heavily. Eleanor often had to find her uncle and take him home. Guests were seldom invited to the house. After one or two unpleasant experiences when Uncle Vallie came home unexpectedly from a spree, only those few who knew the whole situation thoroughly could be made welcome. Otherwise the family was on edge the whole time, anticipating some unpleasant incident with a visitor.

Somehow Eleanor found an inner reserve of

strength to deal with this problem. The only bad effect of the whole experience was to give her, as she said, "an exaggerated idea of the necessity for keeping all of one's desires under complete control."

Eleanor's life was now rather lonely. Maude was married and lived many miles away. Eddie, also married, still had an itching foot and was away hunting big game much of the time. And the beautiful, artistic, but very temperamental Pussie, "almost a genius in many ways," was just another child to be cared for. Men were constantly in love with Pussie—"not always wisely, but always deeply"—and she lived from one emotional crisis to another, threatening to jump overboard while on a ship coming home from Europe, locking herself in her room for days without eating, weeping wildly by the hour.

Then, too, the care of her young brother, Hall, had passed almost entirely into Eleanor's hands. Grandmother Hall, with so many other worries about her family, was completely unfit to take care of a growing boy. Eleanor enrolled him in Groton and, although she had many other things on her mind, managed to visit him regularly.

None of this was good preparation for the gay and joyous debutante Eleanor was expected to be. But

Grandmother Hall saw that her name was put on the "right lists," and Eleanor went to all parties, accompanied by a maid. It took only one party to convince Eleanor that she would never be a popular debutante. It didn't surprise her, but it made her life more difficult. All the other women in her family had been real belles; but she was a tall, gangly, shy wall-flower. But, for all her lack of social success, Eleanor was at an age when she dreaded being left out of things. She was still haunted by her upbringing and believed that what was known as "New York Society" was really important.

The only parties at which she had any real fun were the informal studio ones given by artist friends. At these parties she became better acquainted with her distant cousin, Franklin Roosevelt. They enjoyed their many talks together so much that Franklin didn't even mind that she knew more about some subjects than he did. She had read a great deal, as he had, and he admired her original thinking. He was a very popular young man with charm, good looks, good family background, and an independent income. He had many friends and knew many pretty girls, but rather to his surprise, he found that he was developing for his shy, intellectual cousin a strong affection, a combination of tenderness and admiration.

Franklin found that he missed her unreasonably when they were separated for long months. Nothing seemed to be much fun, not even sailing in his beloved boat, without Eleanor there to share the sport.

After a year of unsuccessful social whirl, Eleanor's common sense luckily came to the rescue, and she decided not to waste a second year doing social rounds, but turned to Junior League activities. She taught calisthenics and dancing at the Rivington Street Settlement House, and although she was often terrified by the sight of men staggering out of saloons, as she went home at night by streetcar, she kept at it doggedly. Once she let Franklin, then a senior at Harvard, meet her at the settlement and squire her home.

As a deb, she also helped the women of the Consumer's League in one of their projects investigating working conditions in garment factories. She was blushing but firm, as she asked to be shown the "plumbing." Thus, she did the routine charitable work of her social group which was expected of her, but it was not what she wanted to do.

Eleanor received her own money when she was nineteen—that second winter back home—but knew absolutely nothing about how to manage it. She had been brought up in a very impractical way, as all girls were then. She ran up bills she couldn't pay because, although she had ample funds, she didn't know how to balance a budget. She didn't know how much she could spend for what. A sympathetic cousin took her in hand and showed her how to keep books. It took her a year to straighten out her bills. This hard but valuable lesson stuck with her so well that afterward, even when she had secretaries who could do it, she always insisted on paying her own bills and checking her own bank statement.

Girls in those days were brought up in a strict formality which seems ridiculous to us now. No girl showed any liking for a man until he had made all the advances. Letters were not exchanged until the young people knew each other very well, and were addressed stiffly and formally "Miss" or "Mr." and signed "Very sincerely yours." A nice girl never allowed a man to give her a present other than flowers, candy, or perhaps a book. If she received a piece of jewelry from a man before she was engaged to him, she ran the risk of being considered "fast," and as for allowing him to kiss her before they were engaged—that was unthinkable.

COMING OF AGE

It was a wonder that young people ever became well enough acquainted with each other to think of marriage—but they did. And Franklin asked Eleanor to marry him.

"I have only a few bright hopes right now," he told Eleanor modestly. And she answered, "I have faith in you; I'm sure you'll really amount to something some day."

When her grandmother asked her if she were in love with Franklin, Eleanor solemnly answered "Yes," although she really had no conception of what being in love meant. She realized that years later, when the added growth and maturity which came with a good marriage showed her the difference between an adult love and the childish emotion she had thought of as love.

The main reason Eleanor was so ready to rush into a youthful marriage, although she didn't realize it at the time, was that she had a great deal of curiosity about living and wanted very much to enjoy every experience. She had never had a home of her own to live in for any length of time, and the thought of having one now appealed to her immensely. She had a strong desire to be a woman, to take a woman's part in the world, and marriage seemed the natural thing.

She had very high ideals about marriage and the rôle of a wife and mother, but almost no knowledge of either. No one bothered to enlighten her.

Many eyebrows in society must have been elevated in surprise that a social failure like Eleanor had made such a "catch," for Franklin Roosevelt was very desirable in the eyes of debutantes and their mothers. He was aristocratic, handsome, wealthy, with a large estate on the east bank of the Hudson, near Hyde Park. At twenty-one he was a self-confident and gay young man. Eleanor's lack of beauty had not prevented her from attracting the most personable young man, with the best prospects, of anyone in their circle of acquaintances.

A casual observer would have said that these two young people had little in common. But basically they had many similar ideas and interests, and it was these which brought them together and set them apart from other young people in their social group. Both had traveled widely, both were interested students of history, both loved literature and knew it well. They differed from the rest of their acquaintances whose main interests were the round of social events and fashionable sports. They really liked the same things and spoke the same language.

Then, too, the very fact that they differed in character made them creative influences in each other's lives. She had not been spoiled enough in her muddled childhood and was consequently a lonely, introspective, and very responsible young woman. He had always had everything he wanted, and he had a personality that drew people to him. There was no doubt that they would be good for each other.

Because they were both so young, it was decided that they should wait a year before becoming formally engaged. Franklin went on a cruise to the West Indies, and Eleanor stayed in Washington with her Auntie Bye.

She had a wonderful winter, meeting young diplomats and officers in the army and navy, who squired her around to the various social functions. Eleanor particularly enjoyed the stimulation of her aunt's vivid personality. Auntie Bye was always the center of any group. Her judgment was sound, her counseling the kind to which young people listened readily. She gave reassurance to her shy niece many times. One particular piece of advice, in which Eleanor found the strength she needed many times in her later life, was given her by this astute friend: "No matter what you do, some people will criticize you. If you are entirely sure that you would not be ashamed to explain your action to some one whom you loved, and you are satisfied in your own mind that you are doing the right thing, you need not worry about criticism, nor feel any need to explain what you do." This became a code for Eleanor, who in her lifetime has probably received more criticism than any other woman.

The following year Franklin came back from his cruise with feelings unchanged, and Eleanor was as eager to marry him as ever. Their engagement was announced and Franklin took Eleanor to meet his family. Eleanor liked the feeling of security she found there, the family solidarity, the level business sense that made them watch their pennies in little things so they could be generous in big things. It was the exact opposite of the home in which she had grown up with Grandmother Hall, where there was no security, only a continual wasting away of a sizeable fortune.

Franklin and his fiancée traveled together to Washington to attend Theodore Roosevelt's inauguration as president of the United States. These two interested young people sat in a family group on the Capitol steps, and watched intently while Uncle Ted raised his right hand and took the oath of office.

COMING OF AGE

"My, I'm glad we're here to see this," Eleanor whispered excitedly to Franklin, "there will never be another event like this in our family!"

And Franklin nodded agreement.

4

MARRIAGE AND A FAMILY

ST. PATRICK'S Day dawned cool and bright. The crowds started gathering early along Fifth Avenue to watch the parade. In the built-up reviewing stand, decorated with many flags, high-ranking military officers and other dignitaries looked out over the heads of the people. Everyone was waiting for President Theodore Roosevelt. Emerald banners bobbed up and down all along the street and the brass band loudly played "The Wearing of the Green."

The hurry and bustle of last minute preparations for a wedding were under way at Cousin Susie's large house, with its two entrances, one on Fifth Avenue and one on Madison Avenue.

As soon as Uncle Ted finished reviewing the St. Patrick's Day parade he made his way, beneath the striped canopy entrance, into the house. He was now ready for the second important function of this day—

giving Eleanor in marriage to Franklin. The gray-helmeted, frock-coated police guarded Uncle Ted so carefully that many of the guests, in shiny new toppers or cartwheel hats, had trouble getting into the house. A few latecomers were delayed so long at the door that they didn't get inside until the marriage ceremony was over.

Eleanor, wearing Grandmother Hall's lace, with a delicate web veil draped over a Tudor cap, carried a bouquet of lilies-of-the-valley as she started down the aisle on Uncle Ted's arm. She joined Franklin before the improvised altar at one end of the long drawing room. The bridesmaids, in cream taffeta, followed slowly. Each wore three ostrich feathers in her hair, to signify the Roosevelt crest.

After the ceremony, friends crowded around to wish the bride and groom happiness. Then suddenly the hubbub subsided and the newlyweds found themselves standing alone in the center of the drawing room. From the library across the hall came sounds of laughter and talk, as Uncle Ted held forth with one of his amusing stories. Eleanor was not a bit surprised. This was what always happened when Theodore Roosevelt, idol of the nation, was at any gathering. "We might as well join the crowd," she said simply, and she and Franklin strolled into the library to listen.

The young Roosevelts had a very brief honeymoon at Hyde Park. Franklin soon had to return to New York City to finish his last year of study at Columbia Law School. They settled in a small apartment. Fortunately for Eleanor, who was loth to display her ignorance as a housewife, a competent housekeeper took care of all details. Mending was the only thing required of the new Mrs. Franklin Delano Roosevelt—and that she could do well, thanks to her early experience with dish towel hems and darned stockings.

When law school was over for the summer, the newlyweds went on a real honeymoon to Europe. For the first time in many years, Eleanor Roosevelt had someone to depend on, someone who made all the plans, bought the tickets, decided what was to be done—"and I slipped into this pleasant existence with the greatest of ease."

It was not easy for Eleanor to adjust her intense, shy nature to Franklin's easy-going gregarious one. But some of her shyness gradually wore off as she met a great many different kinds of people during their travels. When there was a lull in the conversation at a dinner or social gathering, she recalled with amusement the formula her two young aunts had given her for promoting small talk: "Start with the alphabet and go right through it. 'A-apple—do you like apples, Mr. Smith? B-bears—are you afraid of bears? C-cats—do you have the usual feeling, Mrs. Jellyfish, about cats?'" Eleanor found she seldom had to resort to these desperate measures for conversation.

On arriving in London, the young couple were horrified to find that, because of their connection with the President's family, they had been given the Royal Suite at Brown's Hotel in London. The sitting room was so large that if Eleanor dared to put any of her possessions on a table or chair, she never could be sure of finding them again. Their pocketbook was not equal to all this splendor, so they soon sought other lodgings.

They went on to Paris, Milan, Venice, and Murano, doing all the things tourists do—taking pictures, sampling strange dishes, visiting all the places they had heard or read about. Eleanor did all the foolish things she had always wanted to do, aided and abetted by her husband, who had a few fancy ideas of his own.

At a dinner in the home of friends in Scotland, the

hostess suddenly turned to Eleanor and asked, "Can you tell me the difference between your state and national governments in the United States?"

Eleanor stammered a few words and blushed with shame. She turned desperately to her husband. He saw her floundering and came to her rescue, explaining in a few brief sentences, the basic differences in the two forms of government.

When he had finished, Eleanor said to her hostess, "I'm so ashamed. My Uncle Theodore Roosevelt is president of the United States and one-time governor of New York and I can't even answer a simple question about my country's government. As soon as I get home," she added sternly, "I'm going to do something about my ignorance."

Franklin's mother had already rented a home for them on East 36th Street, furnished it, and hired servants before the young couple arrived home from Europe. Eleanor, conscious of her own inexperience and lack of knowledge in such matters, allowed her mother-in-law to take over. Mrs. Roosevelt did not live with the young couple, but hers was the guiding hand throughout their first years of marriage. She was a strong-willed woman with a great deal of managerial ability. There must have been many times when Eleanor justly resented this management, but she never uttered a word of criticism in public. She always spoke kindly of her mother-in-law and kept family affairs to herself.

The following May, a child was born. They named her Anna Eleanor after her grandmother and her mother. Eleanor, knowing absolutely nothing about handling and feeding a baby, hired a young and inexperienced baby nurse, who proved to be more hindrance than help to the bewildered young mother.

She would come running into Eleanor's room. "Miz Roosevelt, Miz Roosevelt, the baby has a rash. Come quick. I think maybe she has exanthema." An hour later she'd come running again. "I was giving the baby a bath and I noticed a mark on the back of her neck—I'm sure she has——" and she would name some obscure ailment. She was always watching the baby for strange symptoms and usually finding them. This, of course, kept the baby's mother in a constant frenzy, until she finally got rid of that nurse and replaced her with a cheerful, motherly woman.

For the next ten years Eleanor Roosevelt "was always just getting over a baby or preparing to have one," as she put it. Each baby meant months of misery to a woman of robust health and energy, who had hardly known a day of sickness in her life. But she didn't let illness prevent her from performing her duties. Undoubtedly she overdid this hard self-discipline, for she said later that she wouldn't recommend it for anyone else. "What it really does is to kill a certain amount of your power of enjoyment. It makes you a stoic, and you tend to draw away from other people, into yourself." Eleanor Roosevelt, in these first years of marriage, was withdrawing more and more into her own shell.

After the second baby, James, was born, Franklin's mother decided that their house was too small, so she bought a plot of land and had a larger one built for them. Eleanor Roosevelt took little interest in these plans and left everything to her husband and his mother.

She still suffered from the extreme sensitivity which had haunted her childhood, and every attempt she made to overcome it seemed to boomerang. She ran the family's first car into a gatepost and was distressed out of all proportion to the incident, refusing to have anything more to do with driving.

Her experience with horses was no better. Unsuspecting, she mounted one which had been trained, by a previous rider, to start running at a certain place, not to stop until he reached another place. One ride, during which she clung desperately to the horse's neck, was enough for Eleanor, who had always been terrified at uncontrolled high speed.

Again, when she found she was a dub at golf, she gave it up and was so discouraged she didn't try any sport for many years.

Her third child died when only a few months old. This added to Eleanor Roosevelt's melancholy and sensitivity. She felt the baby might have lived if she had only taken better care of him—a feeling any mother might have had in the same situation. It's no wonder that at times she had what she called "Griselda moods," during which she crawled into a spiritual hole and pulled it in after her.

Eleanor Roosevelt gradually built up a wall around herself which almost completely isolated her from the rest of the world. She even gave up her interest in personal social work because her mother-in-law told her she might carry disease from the slums to her own children.

Had she kept on like this, her feelings of inferiority would soon have buried her deep in a rut, where all individuality was lost. But the tide suddenly turned, and Eleanor pulled herself out of her hole by sheer force of will.

A strong sense of duty was the first rung on the ladder by which Eleanor climbed up into the daylight of the outside world, into a life crowded with a multitude of interests and activities. Franklin Roosevelt was elected to the state Senate just after Elliott was born. He was now deep in politics, and since she felt it was a wife's duty to be interested in her husband's work, Eleanor allowed herself to be drawn into politics. As easily as that, she began the dual existence which was to last the rest of her life—a public life versus a private one. For as her interest in politics awakened, although she was perfectly certain she "had nothing to offer of an individual nature," she found in public service the satisfactions she needed for a well-rounded life.

At first, her interest in political questions of the day was little more than reflex action and puppet thinking. When her husband made it known that he was strongly in favor of woman suffrage, Eleanor, even though she had never given the question any serious thought, decided that she, too, favored votes for women. Fortunately, she had too keen a mind to be

MARRIAGE AND A FAMILY

satisfied for long with this robot reasoning. "I was beginning to realize," she said, "that something within me craved to be an individual." Thus she gradually emerged from her years of hibernation to take part in the affairs of her country, and became an influence in the lives of her fellow men which has seldom, if ever, been equalled by any woman.

President Woodrow Wilson appointed Franklin Roosevelt Assistant Secretary of the Navy in the spring of 1913, and the family, with Franklin Jr. now added to it, moved to Washington.

Eleanor accompanied her husband on official trips to inspect Navy yards all around the country. They frequently attended late affairs, and had to catch trains and boats at any hour of the day or night. "I was amazed at my own endurance, which had never been really tested in any way before. This was my first realization that, if I had to, I could keep going long after I was tired."

Back home in Washington, Eleanor Roosevelt saw her family through the usual processions of childhood sicknesses. A nation-wide influenza epidemic hit her household hard. At one time there were nine people in the house down at once, and Eleanor had to take care of the sick. "What one has to do, can be done," she said simply, as she put ice caps on feverish heads, sprayed throats, bathed, fed, and entertained almost single-handed, three servants, four children, and her husband in various stages of illness.

All family crises were not so serious, although there were bound to be many minor ones in a household of small boys, aided and abetted by an older sister. Eleanor occasionally had to step in to smooth out strained relations with the neighbors. For instance, the children thought it was fun to drop paper bags, filled with water, from the second-story window. They liked the stir it created among the pedestrians passing by in the street below. She quickly put a stop to this bit of mischief which threatened to sever diplomatic relations with other people living on the same block.

Franklin Roosevelt rarely knew about such smaller happenings until they were all over. Eleanor believed in handling these details herself, so that the house of a public official would run smoothly. They both agreed that their personal life must be somewhat subordinated to public duty.

World War I pushed Eleanor Roosevelt into her first real work outside the family. Increased responsibility brought greater self-confidence. She presided at Red Cross canteens and, as wife of the Assistant Secretary of the Navy, she visited the wounded in Naval hospitals. Horror-struck by conditions in one hospital where shell-shocked Navy men were confined, she reported back to her friend, the Secretary of the Interior. "They are never let out for a breath of fresh air, because of a lack of attendants. They are left behind bars without any attention," she told him. The Secretary appointed a committee to investigate, and more money was appropriated for the hospital, so that conditions could be corrected. Eventually, this Washington hospital became a model for the country.

All this contact and association with many kinds of people was teaching Eleanor Roosevelt to be less severe in her judgments. Her rigid standards were fast disappearing.

After the war was over, Eleanor Roosevelt knew she had to do some useful work. Her war activities had made "social tea living" intolerable. She began, systematically, to prepare herself more adequately for what she wanted to do, both in her home and outside. She went to business school to study typing and shorthand. She also took cooking lessons. She asked less advice from her relatives, asked fewer questions of her friends, and gave fewer confidences to her mother-in-law. She emerged from the war years a new woman in many ways, with a different set of values and a new interest in the world outside her home.

Eleanor Roosevelt's first active work in politics was with the League of Women Voters, in 1920. Working with a woman lawyer, she studied the Congressional Record, bills, and committee reports, and analyzed them for members. Her mother-in-law felt that Eleanor was not sufficiently conscious of her social obligations and objected to her spending so much time on other activities. But Eleanor disliked the type of good works which meant serving on boards, with no personal contact with the people she was helping. She was fast getting away from her conventional class life. She was thinking things out for herself as an individual. She made mistakes, of course, but even these she couldn't regret, because they all added to her understanding of human beings, making her a more tolerant, understanding, and charitable person.

In her next political job, as chairman of the finance committee of the Women's Division of the Democratic State Committee, Eleanor Roosevelt created quite a stir. She was the first volunteer they'd ever had who took her job seriously enough to attend regularly to her duties. These consisted of anything from licking stamps for the volume of mail that went out all over the state, to entering boldly even Republican strongholds to organize women voters in the country. She aroused the interest of other women in campaigning and elections. She organized women who had never before taken an interest in political work of any kind. She also took an active part in the Women's Trade Union League and the Consumer's League.

Although she never demanded equal opportunities for women in the Democratic party, she worked hard to get them. One time, when a party leader refused to see her, she staged a sit-down on his front steps. His wife told her he wasn't in, but Eleanor felt sure he was. "I'll just wait here until he comes," she said.

"I don't know when he'll be back," the wife came out to tell her an hour later.

"It doesn't matter," Eleanor said pleasantly. "I haven't anything else to do. I'll wait."

The woman went back into the house, and a few minutes later the man Eleanor Roosevelt wanted to see came to the door, looking rather sheepish. What was happening to the shy, timid girl?

Then Franklin Roosevelt was stricken with infantile paralysis. The doctor's prognosis was not optimistic. Eleanor learned that her husband might be paralyzed in both legs, relegated to a wheel chair—just at the start of his law career. On the other hand, the doctor admitted that if he had the stamina for a long, hard fight, Franklin might regain partial use of his limbs.

Eleanor Roosevelt knew her husband would fight if there was even a ray of hope. During her visits to the hospital she noticed how hungry he always was for news of the outside world and how much the brief visits of his political friends stimulated his mind and energies.

Eleanor Roosevelt fought hard to carry out her conviction that her husband was not going to be an invalid, and should not be treated as one. She and Franklin's mother faced each other across the desk in the doctor's office. The older woman broke the silence first: "Dr. Draper, I'm sure you will agree with me that Franklin will be an invalid the rest of his life. He should, therefore, be retired to a wheel chair. Every precaution should be taken to protect him from excitement and over-stimulation," she said forcefully.

The doctor turned to Eleanor, "And you don't agree—" his raised eyebrows expressed interest.

"I'm sorry, but I don't," she said gently. "I know my husband well enough to feel that this would be the worst thing you could do to him. He is not an invalid. A renewed interest in life is what he needs. Association with his friends and as much activity as he can stand, as his strength comes back, will be the best thing in the world for him."

"I ought to know what is best for my only son," Franklin's mother said firmly. "These political friends of his will sap his strength. He needs rest and complete quiet."

Eleanor Roosevelt turned to the doctor. "We must do what you think best, of course, Doctor Draper. But believe me,"—her hand shook as she leaned forward in her chair, gesturing for emphasis—"if you relegate my husband to the wheel chair now, and forbid him the interests he needs to stimulate his mind, you will be making him an invalid for life. If he fights, he may conquer this handicap. If he gives up . . ." she left the sentence unfinished and sank back into the chair. She was worn out from making this fight, on top of weeks of strain and worry.

The silence in the office was louder than any noise as Dr. Draper gazed thoughtfully out of the window. He turned around slowly in the swivel chair and faced the two women. "You're right,"—he looked straight at Eleanor—"his recovery will be speeded if he takes part in public affairs again. You can do many of the heavier tasks for him. But he is not an invalid, and there is no reason why he should be treated as one."

Eleanor Roosevelt felt that it would help her husband most if she began some public work of her own, that her immediate duty was to act as her husband's connecting link with the world, while he made his long, tedious fight back to an active life. So, while he recovered in health and gradually regained partial use of his legs at Warm Springs, Georgia, Eleanor bought a third interest in the Todhunter School in New York. As vice-president of this fashionable school for girls, she taught civics and literature classes. Later, she felt, would be time enough for her to go more directly into politics.

Her school teaching was practical and concrete. One course, called "Happenings," was given to an informal group of sixteen-year-old girls seated around a table with her. They discussed items in the daily papers and their significance to the individual. Eleanor Roosevelt did everything she could to make history, elections, and various functions of the government something alive and of vital importance to each of them, something closely related to their daily lives.

She took them to see the line-up at police headquarters, and they asked questions in the darkened room while bright lights centered on suspects. She took them to see the police call set-up and all of the city's machinery for crime prevention and control.

While Franklin Roosevelt fought his battle against illness, his wife waged a personal war on the home front. She knew that if her children were going to learn to ride and swim, and carry on the other normal activities of childhood, she would have to do these things with them, since their father could no longer take part in these activities. It wasn't easy. First of all, her old lack of self-confidence in driving a car came back to haunt her, but she kept at it until she could chauffeur the children from place to place. She went to the Y.W.C.A. and took swimming lessons, conquering her old fear of the water by sheer force of will. And she resumed the horseback riding she had discontinued years before.

"If the children were going to have a normal existence without a father to do these things with them, I had to become a good deal more of an all-round person than I ever had been before," she said, as she continued her program of learning new sports along with her children.

On Campobello Island, New Brunswick, the Roosevelts owned a spacious summer place. This became the vacation site for all the young Roosevelts while they were growing up, and later a honeymoon cottage for each of the children in turn. Eleanor felt that this Canadian "cottage" of three stories, green lawns, and tennis courts, was just the place for her family at this time.

From this base she branched out on camping trips with two or more of the children. When Franklin Jr. cut himself with a hatchet, she administered first aid. When it was time to build a fire for a cook-out, she helped gather wood and construct a stone fireplace. When it was time to go swimming Eleanor was the first one to jump into the cool green waters of Passamaquoddy Bay.

Particularly interesting to the children were the rides on the back of a small burro they had added to the Roosevelt menage. They held their sides and

MARRIAGE AND A FAMILY

shrieked with laughter when the burro insisted on lying down and trying to roll every time their mother got on his back.

Another difficult problem which Eleanor Roosevelt had to face during the long period of strain following her husband's illness was her teen-aged daughter's misunderstanding. Anna did not realize that her mother was harried by family complexities and the anxiety of illness. She was convinced her mother didn't care for her because she had so little time for her these days. Eleanor, on her part, did not understand how very unhappy the girl was as a day-student in a boarding school. "It took a little while to realize that my attitude toward Anna was all wrong. I still thought of her as a child and treated her as one. It never occurred to me to take her into my confidence and consult her about our difficulties."

Under the strain of one particularly hard day, Eleanor broke down in a fit of hysteria. This brought hidden difficulties out into the open. Anna, after offers of help, very sensibly left her mother alone, and as Eleanor said with her usual frankness about herself, "I soon got over it when everyone left me alone. An emotional jag usually requires an audience."

When she had recovered, Eleanor Roosevelt sat

down with her daughter and had a long talk. Anna poured out her fears, and they ironed out all their misunderstandings. Anna and her mother have been close friends ever since—all the more, perhaps, because their comradeship developed so slowly.

5

"ELEANOR AND I"

THE next few years were full for Eleanor Roosevelt. She realized that if her husband was to have a political career to come back to, she would have to keep his name before the public. This she did, though it involved considerable speech-making, which she hated. Consequently, in 1924, when Franklin Roosevelt, still in a wheel chair, was ready to go back into politics, he found himself only a little behind, despite his long illness. He began a campaign which resulted in his election, in 1928, as governor of New York.

The Roosevelts became a team, working side by side in all things. Eleanor Roosevelt had her own activities and interests, of course, and her husband had duties which she could not share, but their two lives were woven into a closely knit pattern of family unity, personal development, and service to their country. They had a fine working companionship, built upon confidence in each other's ability. The individual accomplishments of either of them are unique and outstanding—but even greater was the work they did together as a team.

After he was elected governor of New York, Franklin Roosevelt made a round of the state hospitals, homes for the aged, prisons, and reform schools. Since he could not walk through these institutions, his wife became his eyes and ears. After her first visit to a home for the aged, he fired a dozen questions at her: "How good was the plumbing in the kitchen? Were the menus posted there? Did they show a balanced diet? Was the medicine cabinet well stocked? Was the first-aid room spotless? What kinds of recreation were provided for the old folks?"

"Why I don't know," his wife answered. "I never thought to look." Under her husband's instruction she soon learned to poke and peer into dark corners to get all the answers. She used her eyes and ears to good advantage.

Although she had come a long way since her first "blushing experiences" as a Junior Leaguer, this prying to uncover concealed facts, to look in the more obscure places for negligence and dishonesty, was still repulsive to her. She realized, however, that if public institutions were to be properly run and the people living in them fairly treated, such work was necessary. It was a valuable education for someone who had, for the most part, been sheltered from the unpleasant side of life.

Eleanor Roosevelt's name never appeared in any of the political work which eventually promoted Franklin Delano Roosevelt to President, but her shrewd planning was there—a telling factor in the campaign. She was especially interested in explaining the workings of democracy to women. This won many staunch supporters for her husband's career. Her graphic description of governmental investigations into dark closets made more than one newspaper editorial give vigorous support to the President.

No woman has done more to promote universal suffrage and to encourage women to take an active part in the government of their country. "Democracy means that you use your ballot, that you join the political party you believe in, and that you work in the party to get better candidates," Eleanor Roosevelt said over and over again to women's clubs and civic groups.

Eleanor Roosevelt made a valiant effort, at first, to stay out of politics in her husband's campaign, but she was relentlessly drawn in. If she accepted or refused an invitation to a tea, it was construed as political opinion for or against that group. When asked to speak, she always tried to make it clear that she was not speaking as the wife of a political candidate—and later, not as the wife of the President. This did no good. No matter how many times she denied it, most people were sure that her remarks indicated definite political opinions of the President.

After Franklin Roosevelt was elected to the Presidency, Eleanor Roosevelt became her husband's special emissary, searching for facts in far corners of the world. More and more she became the President's representative, the one person he could trust to give an unbiased report on real conditions.

The phrase "Eleanor and I" was often on Franklin Roosevelt's lips. Never were there two people in the White House who knew more about what was going on in their country than the Roosevelts. She reported the facts accurately. For the most part they agreed on what the end result should be. Even when the President did not agree with her on the best way to accomplish an objective, he respected her opinions and motives. Eleanor Roosevelt seldom gave the President advice, but on those rare occasions when she

"ELEANOR AND I"

did, it was strong enough to command his attention.

"Franklin," she would say, "before you pass judgment on that new Moore Bill before Congress, I think you ought to hear what Watson Hill has to say. After all, he's been making a special study of that type of legislation for years. I believe he could throw some new light on the whole matter. Wouldn't you like to talk with him?"

The Roosevelts' teamwork was vigorous and fruitful. She not only did the President's footwork, but also deliberately created, each day in her home, the atmosphere that a harried and hard-working executive needed. She completely changed the average citizen's idea of what a President's wife should be. The ranks of those who said, "Why can't the President's wife stay in the White House and just be a gracious hostess?" were steadily decreasing.

Often the request came from one group or another, "If we can't have President Roosevelt to make a speech at our meeting, may we have Mrs. Roosevelt instead?"

She read drafts of his important speeches and many changes were made at her suggestion. He encouraged her to express her opinions even when he knew they differed greatly from his. Eleanor Roosevelt had the importance of a cabinet member without portfolio. She was rapidly becoming the most influential woman of our time. To sophisticated politicians, her simplicity was unbelievable. They thought it a disguise for political cleverness and were always looking for some hidden meaning in her words, some straw in the wind that would point to a decision on a governmental issue.

Many times she parried the questions of smart politicians, who were trying to get advance information on some policy the President was considering. Because she wanted to express her own personal opinion without reflecting government policies or plans, she would say, with a twinkle in her eye, "No one ever tells me anything."

When prohibition was repealed, everyone was very curious as to whether alcoholic beverages would be served in the White House. Eleanor Roosevelt was well-known as a teetotaler, so the newspapermen asked the President. "You'll have to ask my wife," he said. The next day reporters, meeting her at the airport as she returned from New York, asked her the same question. "You'll have to ask my husband," she answered. When she heard what the President's answer had been, she laughed. "I guess we'll have to consult together and answer your question at the next press conference," she said.

The most endless question of all was, "Is Mr. Roosevelt going to run for President again?" She must have heard that one a thousand times. She developed a stock answer. "I've never asked him—you might, if you get the chance," she would say calmly. One time a brash young man, trying a new approach —he thought—asked what she expected to be doing after November. She smiled appreciatively. "Young man, that is the cleverest way of asking the same question I've ever heard," she said.

Someone once asked her, "Do you feel your husband would have been the truly great man he was had he not been stricken by infantile paralysis?" Eleanor Roosevelt answered, "It depends on the individual's strength of character, and ability to use to good advantage whatever happens to him in life. My husband accepted infantile paralysis as a challenge. Discipline and overcoming suffering have helped to make him the great individual he has become."

Time after time Eleanor Roosevelt had to deny that she was a possible candidate for office herself. Many Americans, even those against a third term for President Roosevelt, were in favor of one for her. There were even some who felt that she would make a fine president herself. "Mrs. Roosevelt," they said, "has a better understanding of the needs of her countrymen and the solution to their problems than most of the politicians in the country." But her answer was always the same: "Nothing could persuade me to run for political office."

She was, however, more than willing to act as her husband's sounding board. He often tried out new ideas on her. "I told my husband that if he could make me understand something, it would be clear to all the other people of the country," she said. Such a statement, in the face of her keen understanding and astute knowledge of all that goes on in this country, is the epitome of modesty.

Perhaps the greatest service she performed for the thousands of people who trusted her and valued her opinions, was to keep the President in their midst. She never let him become an isolated figurehead in Washington. She brought their needs and thoughts close to him. She transported the President to the people. Eleanor Roosevelt's simple, friendly manner, which made farmer's wives say, "She's a fine lady—just as homey as we are," prevented people from being overawed by the pomp and circumstance which surround the President of the United States.

She chatted with them on buses; she talked with workers and housewives in small towns. Very few asked any more, "Why must she go around sticking her nose into everything?" The reasons were self-evident. In fact, as time went on they asked her to come more and more. Her traveling caused less comment and more admiration. "How does she ever get around so much? Where does she get all that energy?" people would ask as she flew to New York for a women's committee meeting and then, with hardly a pause for breath, caught a train for Washington, to stand beside the President at a diplomatic reception. Later that night, she might board a sleeper for Florida or Maine. Eleanor enjoyed these trips despite the wear and tear. She wanted to escape any "featherbed" kind of existence. Here was one First Lady who would not stay in the White House and push buttons for anything she wanted.

Her naturalness and warmth won over everyone, even those who were strongest in opposition to "New Deal" policies. One time she attended a tree planting ceremony led by a staunch Republican lady. "I've never met Mrs. Roosevelt, but really, I don't see how I'm going to stand having anything to do with a

Roosevelt," she said before the ceremony. "I suppose I must be civil to her—but that's all!"

It took ten minutes for Eleanor Roosevelt to melt her resistance. "She's really wonderful, isn't she?" the Republican lady murmured to a friend as the ceremony got under way. Somehow Mrs. Roosevelt has that effect on people.

Her husband and family always came first, no matter how many more interests she added to her limitless capacity. She tried to handle family affairs by herself as much as possible, feeling that her husband's mind should be free for other things. Although under no circumstances would she bother him with household details, she thought it important to consider his preferences when any large changes were to be made. "What color do you think the upholstery should be in the living room? Do you think you need new draperies in your study? How about blue and gold, do you think that would look good?"

While Franklin Roosevelt managed the political life, Eleanor held the First Family together. Since, as they grew older, they were very much scattered, this was not easy. It meant frequent long trips, for her children settled in Virginia, Texas, and California, Washington, and Massachusetts.

"ELEANOR AND I"

She had a close relationship with each of her children, and with all her grandchildren as well. Even when they were settled in their own homes, with their own families, some clear across the country, her children called on her first in any emergency. She frequently acted as peacemaker and calming influence in family differences. She would fly out to Seattle to keep a promise to help her grandson celebrate a birthday, as readily as she would travel to Massachusetts, to be on hand if a birth or death occurred in the family. She had no false dignity to keep her from romping with her grandchildren. She got down on the floor and growled like a ferocious lion, or was a bucking bronco, ridden by a small grandson.

Many of her trips were personal, of course, but a larger number of them were on government business. There were many, however, who grouped all her traveling under "pleasure," and criticized her severely. In fact, there were some who criticized everything she did.

During the second World War she was the President's emissary to several war fronts. She visited Puerto Rico and the Virgin Islands, accompanied by a number of newspaperwomen, because Franklin

Roosevelt had suggested that she get a firsthand picture of conditions there. She visited hospitalized marines in New Zealand, aircraft plants in Canada, and plantations in Latin America. She was to give the President an accurate account of conditions in all these places. He knew he could rely on her unbiased report.

These trips were subject to many attacks by political enemies; so was the promotion or appointment of any Roosevelt. There were many cries of favoritism. A few unreasonable people went so far as to say it was strange that none of them was hurt in the war.

This last straw made one son write home, "Sometimes I almost hope that one of us gets killed so maybe they'll stop picking on the rest of the family."

And always, the First Lady bore the main attack. She had made a trip to the South Pacific, a hard and dangerous one. She dreaded it, but her conscience made her go. It was called a pleasure trip—this journey through mine-filled seas and over besieged islands. But letters from lonely G.I.'s after she returned home, saying, "You did more for our morale than half a dozen U.S.O. shows," made up to her for all the unfair criticism.

In the fall of 1942 she decided to go to England,

and visit troops. She felt she should go even though she was just recovering from influenza. She visited twenty-six groups in ten days—a terrific job even if she'd felt fine. Army officers were unanimous in their enthusiastic description of her effect on morale.

At home too, she was doing all she could to keep civilian morale high. More and more people were saying to those in trouble, "Why don't you see Mrs. Roosevelt about it?" She had become not only the most active and most widely traveled First Lady, but the most human as well. Someone would write, "Come and let us show you something," and she'd go, time after time, no matter how great the distance.

She had a special sixth sense which guided her in channeling problems through government officials, so that they would not think she was interfering. Most of them considered her a real help. The honest ones, trying to do a good job, were glad to have her call their attention to situations they might not otherwise come across.

One day she sat at her desk in her room at the White House, talking to a middle-aged carpenter from Idaho.

"Mrs. Roosevelt," he said earnestly, "I think you ought to know that there are some underhanded things going on in the government housing project in my town. I helped build these houses for the government, and I know they're good. I want to live in one of them. I can meet all the requirements, and I had my application in early. Last week I was told there is no room for me."

"Are all the apartments filled with tenants?" his listener asked.

"That's just it, Mrs. Roosevelt, they're not. Most of them have stood empty for over a month now. That's what makes me smell a rat."

The next day Mrs. Roosevelt and the carpenter boarded a train for Evansville, Idaho. Two days later she flew back to Washington alone. "I'll do what I can," she had promised her fellow-investigator. He smiled as she waved good-by from the ramp leading to the plane.

Back in Washington, Eleanor Roosevelt went immediately to the official in charge of government housing projects. She never tried to angle through a personal friend. She stated the situation briefly, ending with ". . . and so, because of local politics, these dwellings are vacant and will remain so until the politicians get what they want—unless something is done about it."

The government official exploded abruptly: "It's disgraceful. Something must be done at once. Thank you, Mrs. Roosevelt, for telling me about this." Then in a calmer tone, he added: "Have you any suggestions as to the best way to solve this problem?"

He was grateful to her for showing him a deplorable situation which he might have overlooked in the vast scope of his job. Eleanor Roosevelt sat in his office another hour, discussing a solution to the problem. She left the final action entirely up to him.

She could not, of course, give every problem such individual attention. But she often sent a memorandum to the right person, saying, "Do you think anything can help this situation?" Although she never tried to force action on anyone, many problems received speedier attention because of her interest. If an official decision differed from her own opinion, she said nothing more about it.

Because she always found time to help solve even the smallest human problem, Eleanor Roosevelt became not only the President's partner and a vital force in her country's affairs, but also the beloved personal friend of millions of her countrymen.

6

FIRST LADY

A NEW "first" family moved into the White House in January 1932. The First Lady was a tall, stately woman just one inch short of six feet, erect and graceful. Her soft brown hair was only slightly touched with gray, her blue eyes sparkled with cheerfulness and interest, except when they glowed with anger at injustice. Her long-fingered, expressive hands reflected the tremendous energy felt by everyone who knew her.

Eleanor Roosevelt's enthusiasm and buoyant optimism had won her friends wherever she went. Her graciousness and poise were the result of long, arduous self-discipline. She had conquered obstacles a lesser woman would have found insurmountable. Circumstances which have sunk many a woman into a deep trough of self-pity, drove her to greatness.

And yet, through it all, much still remained of the

girl who had grown up in a time when horse and buggies rode dirt roads. Her simplicity still showed in everything, though she was now First Lady of the land.

As the new mistress of the White House, Eleanor Roosevelt struck a happy balance between making it a comfortable home for her family and the people who worked there, and preserving the traditional First Home of the nation. She made a definite distinction between her family's own private quarters, and the hallowed public section of the White House, where a servant polished the brass rails on the stairway every fifteen minutes during open season. Every month 83,000 casual visitors climbed this stairway.

Although the consent of the Fine Arts Commission was needed to add the smallest piece of furniture to the public section, she made the family part of the White House into a home, stocking it with the personal belongings of a large family.

The President's bedroom was made pleasant with his marine paintings, ship models, and naval prints on the walls and table. Other rooms were liberally sprinkled with family portraits, which were later interspersed with cartoon caricatures of the First Lady at various points in her career. With the background of the Washington monument in the distance, at one side of the house she added a children's sandbox, and had a rope swing hung from one of the stately old trees.

Her practical nature asserted itself as she made the necessary changes. She decided, for instance, that it would be foolish to waste valuable time and energy in moving from place to place while dressing in the huge bedroom usually assigned to the First Lady. So she made this huge room into a study, and the small dressing room next to it became her bedroom.

Even though they now lived in the White House, there was no curbing the lusty Roosevelt clan. Priceless antiques were simply moved out of the way of this large and boisterous family. They enjoyed teasing each other, and a great deal of horse-play went on every time a few of them gathered together. Wherever they met, there were noise, people, and excitement. The children called the President and his wife "Ma" and "Pa," teasing them and each other frequently. Their family conversations would keep one "in stitches." Even the staid butler couldn't keep his face solemn, no matter how hard he tried. This family really enjoyed itself.

Large changes in the interior of the White House

were an important decision. Thousands of dollars of public money had to be spent to redecorate even a single room. It became an important matter whether the room should be blue and gold or cream and wine, when it might have to stay that way for twenty years.

Exterior and formal rooms remained the same at the White House, but enormous changes took place elsewhere. One of the rooms on the ground floor was made into a museum for the many beautiful and curious gifts sent to the Roosevelts during their years in the White House. A swimming pool was installed in the basement floor of the west wing and air conditioning was added to most parts of the White House. A shooting gallery was built under the long east entrance, where the Secret Service men often practiced pistol shooting. Secret Service men guard the White House night and day. Strangely enough, the President is the one person in the country who has no key to his own front door.

On her first official tour of her new home, Eleanor Roosevelt learned that the little economies practiced in any home were also practiced there. The curtains were turned, tablecloths darned, worn rugs rewoven or mended. At least a million people a year tramped through the White House. No wonder the rugs fell apart! It took the impending visit of the King and Queen of England, however, to get a new rug for Mrs. Roosevelt's room.

Once Eleanor Roosevelt had things running smoothly, she found she need devote only the first fifteen minutes of the day to housekeeping. This was quite a feat, in a household where the wages of the staff alone totaled $100,000 annually, the electric bill $1000 a month, and the laundry bill between $3000 and $5000 a year.

Just the same, she knew what was going on in her household every minute of the day. She knew the exact number of hot dogs needed for a picnic, or the precise seating arrangements of a formal dinner to an ambassador. She had her finger on everything—whether it was 23,000 sandwiches for a tea, or a dinner with 300 guests. Unlike former First Ladies, she never left such planning to servants. She realized her limitations, however. Knowing that she was an executive housekeeper only, with no real housekeeping skills of her own, she wisely left the actual preparations to others.

Her first big dinner was for a group of foreign diplomats, at which ninety-nine people were present. This was the biggest dinner ever given in the White

House up to that time. Formal functions showed more variety under Eleanor Roosevelt's supervision than ever before. When she gave a musicale, for instance, besides the customary classical musicians, a variety of whistlers, minstrels, hillbilly musicians, and even magicians held the spotlight in turn. Some socialites looked down their noses a bit when, on one occasion, a group of cowboys with banjos, guitars and "sweet potatoes" serenaded the King and Queen of England with "Red River Valley." But Their Majesties enjoyed it very much, and the First Lady was giving them a cross section of American music.

The royal visit from England was, perhaps, the biggest social event during Eleanor Roosevelt's years in the White House. "What will I say to Their Majesties?" one of her friends asked excitedly in the midst of preparations.

"Oh, just say 'How do you do,'" Eleanor answered easily. She was the only calm person in Washington at that point.

There were, of course, many social events scheduled during the royal visit, but perhaps the most interesting one was a "New Deal Tea," arranged by Eleanor Roosevelt on the south grounds of the White House. She invited men and women who dealt with problems of education, employment, housing, and labor. John L. Lewis, president of the United Mine Workers, and William Green, president of the American Federation of Labor, were among those invited. The First Lady thought that an affair of this type would give Their Majesties an opportunity to learn more about the United States, its people, and its government than either formal functions or sightseeing tours.

Even on the most formal occasions, with the biggest crowds, Eleanor Roosevelt has a knack for making people feel her personal interest in each one of them. During her busiest moments, she can remember the little things that matter to others. Her retentive and curious mind is quick to recognize even the smallest need of another. In the midst of the hubbub accompanying the visit of the King and Queen of England, she found time to present the six-year-old daughter of one of the cabinet members to Queen Elizabeth. She realized that, for the little girl, it would be an occasion to remember all her life.

Hundreds and hundreds of unofficial guests came to luncheons, teas, and dinners. Guests at informal affairs included many besides the high-ranking members of the Navy, Army, or diplomatic corps. A farm boy and a visiting duke might eat corned beef and cabbage at the same table.

Eleanor Roosevelt took with her to the White House the Sunday night supper custom of scrambling eggs in a chafing dish at the table. At first people looked with disapproval at the sight of the President's wife presiding over a hot chafing dish. But Eleanor saw no reason to change this old family custom they all loved, just because she was now the First Lady.

When she first saw the kitchen of the White House, Eleanor Roosevelt was horrified. There were "dark looking cupboards, sinks with worn wooden drains, and one old wooden dumbwaiter. Rats, cockroaches, ants, and moths shared the living space with thirty-two servants." She was also shocked at the inconveniences with which the servants had to work.

Under her influence, the government appropriated $165,000 to modernize the kitchen. With the improvements she suggested, the servants were no longer forced to stand up during their rest periods, hang their coats in the corridor, or wash their hands at the kitchen sink. They now had lockers, washrooms, and a pleasant rest room. A special ventilating system was installed. She tried to make it "an example of decent living for those who have to work in somebody else's house."

One servant of many administrations, reflecting on the new order of things, sighed, "I don't know what we'll do when Mrs. Roosevelt isn't here any more." Eleanor realized that, while being First Lady was a very temporary condition, these improvements would last long after she had left the White House.

No First Lady ever engaged in such a variety of activities. A summary of a single day in her schedule is almost unbelievable. Up in the morning at 6:00, she went for a ride on horseback, enjoying the early morning stillness and freshness of the park. No matter how late she stayed up the night before, she was always up with the birds. Then she had a brief dip in the White House swimming pool, and answered half of her mail before breakfast. After breakfast came her fifteen-minute conference with the housekeeper.

On one particular morning, at 10:00 A.M. she personally conducted a group of visiting lobstermen from Maine on a tour of the White House. Lobstermen or kings—it made no difference. As their hostess, Eleanor Roosevelt was, as usual, just herself, doing everything she could to make them feel welcome. Evidently she succeeded, too, for as the visitors left the White House she heard one of them say to the other, "She ain't stuck-up, she ain't dressed-up, and she ain't afeared to talk."

At 11:00 A.M. she had her weekly conference with the ladies of the press. She received them in the East Room, beneath the famous portrait of George Washington, the one Dolly Madison tore from its frame and gave to a French butler, when the British burned the White House during the war of 1812. The room matched the First Lady's graciousness and dignity. Four mirrors above the fireplaces, a grand piano, and a few gold brocaded benches against the wall were the only furnishings. She greeted them warmly and led them from the formal room into her more informal study.

She sat busily knitting a sweater for one of her grandchildren as she talked, the needles clicking steadily along as she answered questions. Once in a long while she smoked to be companionable. But she did it so badly that it provided grist for the mill of the cartoonists, who certainly found Eleanor Roosevelt an abundant source of inspiration.

"What are you going to wear to the Senate wives' luncheon today?" one reporter asked.

"I hadn't really thought about it," she answered

reflectively. "But let me see, I might as well make up my mind right now—I think I'll wear the blue crepe with the lace collar." Then she launched into an extemporaneous discussion of a new tax bill being considered in Congress.

At one o'clock she gave a luncheon for fifty Senate wives, with a musicale afterward. Then at three, she hopped a train to Baltimore to investigate conditions in some cotton mills there. She was back in time for a family dinner, and stood in the receiving line for a formal ball that evening. Between these activities of the day, though it is impossible to imagine where she fitted them in, she planned menus for two forthcoming luncheons, answered a considerable volume of correspondence, made any number of appointments for future events by telephone, and talked with one of the government agencies about a needy family in Arkansas.

Only her abundant health and stamina could have kept her feeling fit through all these activities. Her reputation for never missing a social function was so great that, when on one occasion she failed to come to an important diplomatic dinner, everyone was deeply concerned. The guests were relieved but puzzled when she turned up later in the evening for the musicale, and shook hands with all of them. The word went around that she had had a headache. However, since Eleanor Roosevelt had never in her life given a headache excuse for being absent from anything, this didn't satisfy her friends.

Eventually the real story came out. At dinner the tables had been arranged in the horseshoe customarily used so that no guest would have his back to the President. If Eleanor Roosevelt had been there, the President's mother, having no official rank, would have been forced to sit way down at one end of the long table. Eleanor, with her innate kindness and foresight, had absented herself from dinner, thereby making Mrs. Roosevelt the hostess of the occasion, sitting directly across from the President.

Being a good hostess at any time is an art, Eleanor Roosevelt thinks, built upon tact and consideration of others. It must be combined, however, with an ability to make the wheels go around smoothly without too much fuss. You'd think she would resent the countless hours spent standing in line and shaking hands with thousands of people, but she doesn't at all. One day she shook hands with 1725 Democratic ladies at 1:30, and then with 1500 members of a ladies' auxiliary at 3:00.

"I nearly always learn something new from every one of them," she says. Besides, Eleanor Roosevelt has developed a formula to prevent bottlenecks in the receiving line. It saves wear and tear on her right hand. She grasps each person's hand firmly, and gently draws him past as she smiles and says, "Nice to meet you—how are you?"

Even the least White House visitor, stepping off a train at Washington, was greeted immediately by the First Lady's thoughtfulness. As the train slowed down, coming into the depot, the guest wondered how she could ever find the driver who would take her to the White House. But almost before her foot touched the platform, a man in chauffeur's uniform, with red, white, and blue cord around his hat, greeted her by name. He had been well coached and recognized her instantly.

"And then," as one visitor put it, "I was ushered into her presence, and as soon as she spoke I forgot to feel awed. My knees stopped shaking and I felt at ease. I forgot everything but her charm."

Eleanor Roosevelt's Christmas shopping methods show best her consideration for others in little things. She begins early in the year, and in every place she goes thereafter, she adds to her store of the hundreds of presents she will give the following Christmas. Her shopping is done long before the department stores start warning the public that there are only twenty shopping days left until Christmas.

She often stops to buy a dozen of these presents on the way to a train. She keeps a card index where she lists every gift, so that she won't duplicate. She buys hand-made presents from the blind and handicapped, and sends hundreds of gifts every Christmas to those in need. No one ever spent more time on little presents for the lonely, the needy, and the sick. She sends gifts from whatever place she may be at the moment—oranges from California, pottery from Mexico, some woolens from England.

There is no way of counting the number of people Eleanor Roosevelt has secretly supported. She has a deep dislike of the "lady bountiful" type of charity, dispensed from a distance, usually with the mere giving of money. She feels it is more important to give of oneself—in time, energy, and interest. She believes that the best kind of living is that which helps others learn to help themselves.

Where there is real need, she tries to get at the root of the trouble, not just gloss over it with the indiscriminate handing out of money. Speakers who talk about "the gratitude of the poor" make her squirm. "Why should they be grateful for the little they have?" she says. "It is we, who have so much more, who should be grateful—not condescending."

7

MY DAY

"AND because she has not felt it necessary to retard her efforts to advance the good of humanity just because she happens to be the wife of the President of the United States," the chairman concluded, "I am happy to present to you at this time—Eleanor Roosevelt."

A straight-backed woman with her head held high stood up. Thirty thousand people rose to their feet and clapped and shouted their pride in her. Then a hush settled over the crowd as they sat down again. She hadn't a note in front of her as she began her simple speech. Many eyes were misty before she finished her plea for the homeless. Her dignified appeal reminded them of the privilege it was to be an American, and of the obligation that went with it. As she finished and sat down, there was a prolonged moment of silence, then the applause burst forth. It echoed from the corners of the large hall, thundering down the long aisles; its vibration shook the platform on which she sat.

During her first seven years in the White House, Eleanor Roosevelt delivered several hundred similar lectures, in person and over the radio, wrote a million words, traveled 280,000 miles, and shook half a million hands. She earned, and gave away, more than half a million dollars.

Of all these activities, radio broadcasting probably came hardest to her. When she first faced a microphone she was uneasy and nervous. Her voice had a tendency to rise to high registers and crack at just the wrong moment. With her usual sensible attitude, Eleanor decided to do something about it right away. She took lessons in speech and breath control. Before long only a shadow of those first harrowing broadcasts remained in her easy, pleasant delivery. By writing and rewriting material, and spending long hours rehearsing before the microphone, she gradually developed a fine radio technique. Eleanor Roosevelt started in radio as an unskilled amateur and ended up a skilled professional.

During a broadcast she always massages her hands

as she stands before the microphone. This is not a nervous habit, but just one more example of her amazing ability to utilize her time. She uses these moments to repair the damage involved in shaking hands with thousands and thousands of people.

Her standard rate for a fifteen minute broadcast was $3000 ($500 a minute). In her first six contracts she made about $150,000 and gave all of it to charity. At first, she even paid the income taxes out of her own pocket, so that the entire sum might go to the organizations she felt needed her support. When this became too heavy a burden, she deducted taxes first, then gave away the rest.

While she was First Lady, Eleanor Roosevelt never let her radio programs interfere with her White House duties, or her work with government agencies. When she was working on a government project in some obscure part of the country, far from a radio station, she would deliver her radio program by long-distance telephone. By previous agreement she shared equally, with the sponsor, the cost of this arrangement —as many times as necessary.

Many hundreds of people—friends and strangers —wrote to her, asking her to give up "this public spectacle of herself." "It isn't seemly for the First Lady to do commercial radio work," they said. But she answered over and over again, "The organizations who receive the money I earn from these broadcasts really need it. I think this is more important than any false idea of my own prestige."

Her writings cover even more ground than her radio work. She now enjoys freedom from the restrictions she had as the President's wife, when she was afraid that something she said might be construed as his opinion or idea. Writing is her favorite occupation. She started by writing little essays on White House customs for a newspaper syndicate. As this was not financially successful, the editors suggested she try, instead, a diary called *My Day*.

My Day expanded to appear six days a week in seventy-five newspapers and be read daily by four and a half million people. More women have read her column than any other in any newspaper.

Eleanor Roosevelt has written *My Day* under all circumstances and in every conceivable place, dictating it to her secretary on trains, planes, or sitting by the roadside in a parked car. She has never missed a deadline. One time her editor suggested, "Why don't you take a vacation, like other columnists? You can leave an assistant to do your piece while you're gone; all columnists do it."

She thanked him but said, "No, I like to do this column. I don't want it written by someone else. I'll go on vacation, all right, but I'll mail in *My Day* as usual."

In time this column became very controversial. People were either very much for or very much against it. Some ridiculed its homely philosophy, calling it trivial and ordinary. Others admired it for just these things. As one critic wrote: "*My Day* unfolds some harmless and even banal bits of philosophy. Eleanor Roosevelt sets down trivial and unrevealing details. And yet at the end of it all, it seems clear that here is a discerning observer, a writer who is fascinated by this country, its people, and its problems. She has a vast understanding of the common things of life."

Eleanor Roosevelt's fellow columnist, Westbrook Pegler, thought less highly of her efforts. He did an amusing take-off on her column. In spite of its exaggeration it probably amused her as it did anyone, especially the part which read: "In the afternoon a group of young people arrived at the Little House and we plunged at once into a very interesting discussion of the duty of the citizen, not only towards his country but towards himself and his fellow man in relation to the past and the future ahead.

"One gentleman had rather strong ideas on the subject of nail-biting and while, of course, I realize there are two sides to this question I'm afraid that capital punishment for nailbiters is rather severe. I prefer what seems to me the more democratic way and propose to approach it as a world problem, since nail-biting is not a matter of race or creed."

Unfortunately, Mr. Pegler's remarks about her were not always so harmless and amusing. Often they were untrue and libelous. Friends often urged her to strike back. "At least answer his remarks; don't let people think they're true. He uses you to fill up his column several times a month; why don't you do the same?"

Eleanor Roosevelt couldn't see any sense to that. It wasn't the kind of material she wanted in her column. And she has no spite in her.

"I feel sorry for Mr. Pegler," she said. "I've just about decided that he does what he does because he has to make a living. He can't be a very happy man."

Later she added naïvely, "I've seen Mr. Pegler with his family. Any man who is as kind as he is to his wife can't be wholly bad."

To the majority of people, *My Day* is human and interesting. At first, any controversial and political material was carefully edited out, so there wouldn't be anything in the column "to make people mad." But since argument waxed furiously over the column itself, it seemed futile to worry. Eventually, Eleanor was allowed to include in her column any material she wished.

As time went on she used her column in many different ways, as it suited her purpose. She made vigorous comments on national and international affairs. She denied rumors about her family and answered criticism of her children. Sometimes she even discussed a bill coming up in Congress. But for the most part she stuck to the items her tremendous fan mail showed her the public wanted to read—the details of her daily life.

One year she received 310,000 letters. She personally answered 5000 and signed about 30,000. Her mail still averages several hundred letters a week. Of these, sixty percent are requests for some kind of help. If it is within her power and seems wise, she grants it, whether it is a pair of crutches for a crippled boy in Idaho, or some struggling author's manuscript to be read for criticism and help. Desperate appeals come to her from all over the country. If she can't help personally, she usually finds a friend who can.

In a typical week Eleanor Roosevelt receives ninety-five invitations to go somewhere or do something. This does not include purely social functions. She must turn down about four-fifths of these, because of a fact she has always regretted—that she can not be in more than one place at the same time. One thing is certain, however—her activities are limited only by the indivisibility of the human body.

Four secretaries, including Malvina Thompson—"Tommy," who has been her personal secretary for twenty years—are kept very busy. Her mail includes just about everything, from an invitation to attend an exhibition of ancient bronzes or visit a hospital bazaar, to a spiritualist's offer to put her in contact with her late husband, so that she may have his opinions on world affairs. Each week perhaps a dozen letters will ask her "to devote some thought to" their interests. This might include allowing a figurine of herself to be reproduced in quantity, for the benefit of displaced persons in Europe, or judging an essay contest at the Harper School for delinquent girls.

Once Eleanor Roosevelt has lent her name to any project, no matter what it is, she stays with it and sees it through, if it's humanly possible. She is almost fanatic in obedience to the first rule of conduct for herself: "Engagements must be kept," and just as firm in adhering to her second command: "Mail must be answered."

The only time she did not either personally answer her mail, or have one of her secretaries do it, was after her husband's death. She received 100,000 letters of condolence from other than personal friends, and she acknowledged them all at once with an expression of gratitude in her daily column.

Her other main nonpolitical writings have included several books, temporary editorship of a magazine called "Babies, Just Babies," and, for many years, a question and answer page in a large women's magazine. Most of her questions come from people who deeply trust her and hope she will be able to help them with their problems. Her wisdom, combined with sympathy and understanding, has helped many of them.

In answering questions she relies mostly upon her

common sense and kindliness. Once someone asked, in her *Ladies' Home Journal* page, if she would vote for a Negro for president. This is the kind of slippery problem which asks for trouble, no matter which way it is answered. It was a sticker no one would have blamed her for side-stepping. Eleanor Roosevelt answered it effortlessly. She simply said that she felt a candidate should be considered, not on the basis of creed or color, but on his or her qualifications for the job. She added that she also felt no one should be considered who could not command the support of a majority of the people of the country, because unless he had such support, he would not have the strength to carry out the policies of his party.

Eleanor's inexhaustible energy completely floors her friends. "Hasn't this been a grand vacation?" she says at the end of an exhausting tour, during which she has been reading, knitting, speaking, planning speeches, writing her column, answering her mail, shaking a thousand or so hands, and catching trains or planes. Her traveling companions, too tired even to be disturbed by this remark, look at her hopelessly. Her secretary merely groans.

Besides being a source of amazement to those who work with her, Eleanor Roosevelt's energy is the complete despair of weary newspaperwomen whose job it is to keep up with her comings and goings. There is at least as much truth as humor in the cartoon which appeared in one of the nation-wide newspaper syndicates, under the title: "The Newspaperwomen's Prayer." The caption read: "Dear God, please make Eleanor tired—just for a day."

On one trip, to view a homestead project in Virginia, reporters traveled all night, rose at six in the morning, and motored three-hundred miles to listen to her make fourteen speeches. At the end of the day, desperately tired, they climbed on a train and chatted with her in her compartment until eleven P.M. As she got up from her chair, signifying that the session was ended for the night, one reporter remarked, "Thank you very much, Mrs. Roosevelt, for such a good story. I'm not surprised, though, that you should want to get some rest at last." She sighed tiredly.

Her hostess smiled "Oh," she said quickly, "I'm not going to bed yet. I think I'll do a magazine piece before I turn in. I'm not really tired."

One secret of her tireless energy is that she can dismiss one subject entirely from her mind when she goes on to the next. There are no nagging afterthoughts and worries to bring on fatigue. She often found the drawing room of a train the only place where she could work uninterrupted. Up at 6:30, boarding the train in New York at 7:15, she would work until the train pulled into Washington. During the trip she would have read a conference report on a women's political action group, a pamphlet on education, and a taxation bill due to come up in Congress the next day. She would also have jotted down notes on a book review for the Junior Literary Guild, and outlined a speech for a radio broadcast that evening.

She learned to enjoy hard work. Although she had received none of the training for the working world that most children receive today as a matter of course, she became one of the most energetic and highly paid working women in the world.

At one time, Eleanor Roosevelt was writing three books at once, besides her regular columns and several magazine articles. She was always willing to revise and rewrite an article at the editor's request, and she got them in on time, although sometimes this meant doing the complete job over a week end.

Her literary agent, George Bye, handled all contracts for written material except her regular columns. She never set a price for what she wrote, and did many articles for no fee at all if some small magazine thought her words would help its readers. Mr. Bye usually asked a dollar a word from the large magazines well able to afford it, and all of this money was used for a good purpose.

Eleanor Roosevelt was offered a considerable sum of money to appear in a series of Hollywood shorts, where all she would have had to do was stand and talk, but she refused. The only time she appeared on the screen, except in newsreels, was in a series of three shorts about family hobbies; these included Franklin Roosevelt's ship models and James's collection of historical books. Offers to use her name and picture in advertising came in by the dozens but she refused them all—except one. She allowed her picture to be used, without pay, in an advertisement put out by the airlines to encourage women to travel by air.

The secret of her success in all these fields was her own humility toward each job. She never put on airs or developed temperamental tantrums. She could take constructive criticism and use it for self-improvement. More than one radio technician, used to primadonna tactics, said, after working with her: "She's a sweetheart."

Few people have ever received more criticism,

justified or not, than Eleanor Roosevelt. She has the kind of personality which easily makes headlines. She can not make a little mistake, like anyone else. Her mistakes assume the importance of international incidents. There have always been critics just waiting for her to say something they could pull apart, or for any member of her family to make a false move. In their overzealousness they often manufactured criticism where no basis for it existed.

One time a critic went all-out in denouncing her son Jimmy's drinking. Actually he had a stomach ulcer, and was kept to a rigid soft diet.

"Isn't that ridiculous, when Jimmy can't drink at all," his mother calmly said, when she heard it.

On another occasion, speaking of mistakes she had made with her children, she said simply, "No human being is all-wise, no one lives up to her best all the time. Failure comes to everyone, sometimes."

At first, criticisms bothered and hurt her, but in time she built up an immunity to them. She did what she thought right, in spite of what anyone said. Eleanor Roosevelt learned to laugh things off. No matter how indignant her friends became over some lie that was printed about her, she didn't let it bother her. "It's only the words of those you love which can really hurt you—the rest doesn't matter," she said.

Eleanor Roosevelt herself says that this conditioning to criticism was the greatest personal change she experienced during her years of public life. "To spend your life thinking about what others will say is an unprofitable and embittering existence," she said once, and then added, "but constructive criticism is something else again."

Eleanor Roosevelt knows, better than anyone else, that one can learn from the criticism of those whose judgment you trust. But, most important, you must be your own judge—harder, more exacting, more demanding of yourself than anyone else could possibly be. Eleanor Roosevelt has always been her own severest critic.

Even Westbrook Pegler, after watching her in action, had to say, "There is no other who works as hard or knows the low-down truth about people and the troubles in their hearts as well as she does . . . and she will not have a dollar of profit to show for years of banging around the country on a schedule that would break the mind and body of an old circus trouper."

Someone once sent Eleanor Roosevelt a present of a goldfish bowl. She laughed and said it was very appropriate. "There is, however, one consolation for anyone who lives in the public eye," she added. "While it may be difficult to keep the world from knowing what you eat and what you wear, so much interest is focused on these that you are really left completely free to live your own inner life as you wish. So, if I may offer a thought in consolation to others who have to live in a goldfish bowl it is: Don't worry because people know all that you do, for the really important things about anyone are what they are and what they think and feel, and the more you live in a goldfish bowl the less people really know about you."

8

CHAMPION OF MINORITIES

ELEANOR ROOSEVELT has always championed any group fighting for its rights against public prejudice or indifference. She has real sympathy for the underdog.

Although she has known little poverty or struggle in her own life, she understands the hardships of other people. Despite her background of wealth and aristocracy, she became the champion of the underprivileged and the personal friend of thousands she never met.

Eleanor Roosevelt has fought hard to defend such minority groups as Negroes, newspaperwomen, young people, and farmers. She has worked unceasingly to make jobs and decent living conditions available to miners, factory workers, and married women.

Class discrimination of any kind infuriates her.

Perhaps the group she has most constantly fought and worked for is the Negro race. She has helped improve their hospitals, schools, and homes. She has worked long and hard for the abolition of the poll tax, which takes the vote away from so many Negroes. She has written and spoken often for the passage of an antilynching bill.

Her practical approach to the problem of racial prejudice has accomplished more than any number of high-sounding speeches about "equal rights." She talks to an audience straight from the shoulder: "Lack of education, inadequate housing, poor health facilities, and unemployment for Negroes are a threat to your security, too. Self-interest alone should be enough to compel you to better these conditions. A poor education, and resultant unemployment for the Negro, means lower standards of living for all. You are no less susceptible to the disease bred by inadequate preventive medicine, because your skin is lighter in color. Your child is just as likely to be the victim of an epidemic as the child of your Negro neighbor."

She often quoted Booker T. Washington's phrase: "You cannot keep the Negro in the gutter without getting in there with him." She had no foolish, idealistic dreams of obtaining social equality overnight for the Negro race. "Heredity and environment play a part in everyone's development," she said, "but every human being should have an equal opportunity to make of himself whatever his abilities will allow him to become. Of course you can't force people to accept as friends those for whom they have no liking—race or otherwise. But you can give to everyone in a democracy fundamental rights as a citizen: equality before the law, equality of education, equality to hold a job according to his ability, equality of participation in government through the ballot."

Time after time Eleanor would urge parents not to pass on their racial and religious prejudices to their children. "Children have no bias," she said. "They develop it from adult attitudes. I remember the story of a little white boy who had a Negro playmate. One day his mother, speaking of a neighborhood birthday party, said that of course, his Negro friend couldn't go.

" 'Why not?' asked the little boy.

" 'Well, dear—he's a little different. His skin **is** darker than yours.'

"The little boy looked interested. 'Is it?' he said. 'I never noticed. I'll have to look next time.' "

Another time, in answering a question from a mother who wondered if it were all right for her daughter to go to a dance with a Negro schoolmate, Eleanor Roosevelt said, "If your daughter has known this young boy well, there is no more reason why she should not go with him than with anyone of the other boys whom she knows equally well.

"What lies back of your feeling, of course is the old fear of intermarriage between races. That is something I feel we have to deal with on an entirely different basis from mere friendly association. There may come a time when it will seem as natural to marry a man from any race, or from any part of the world, as it will to marry your next door neighbor.

"However, going to a prom is like any other casual thing which you do; and if we are not going to be able to have ordinary contacts with people who are citizens of our own country, how on earth can we expect that we will be able to have the same kind of contact with people who live in different parts of the world? I would not worry too much about the people with whom your daughter dances. I should hope that she could be unconsciously friendly with all her associates in school, and I would be rather proud that a boy of another race felt that he could ask your daugh-

CHAMPION OF MINORITIES

ter to go to a prom—which shows, I think, that her attitude has been kind and mature."

Not even her worst critic could say that Eleanor Roosevelt lacks the strength to back up her beliefs with consistent action. She has never advised one course of action for others and practiced another herself. In fact, she has always gone much farther in support of her beliefs than she would ask anyone else to go.

When the Daughters of the American Revolution refused the use of their Constitution Hall to singer Marian Anderson, Eleanor Roosevelt resigned from their ranks in the face of scathing public opinion. When she invited a group of delinquent girls to the White House for tea, a majority of the guests were members of the Negro race.

Another time, arriving a few minutes late at a welfare conference in Birmingham, where Negoes were seated on one side of the auditorium and whites on the other, she took a seat on the Negro side. A police officer came over and informed her that there was a city ordinance prohibiting this. The First Lady asked to have a special chair placed for her at the front of the church, and she sat halfway between—just a shade to the Negro side.

Though not a minority in the same sense as the Negro race, newspaperwomen composed another special group which received her championship. She made jobs for many newspaperwomen when such jobs were hard to get. She would not have felt justified in helping women to supplant men on the staffs of newspapers, but, because she was the First Lady to hold press conferences and give out news directly, she created several dozen new jobs—for women reporters only. As long as newspapers employed so few women, she thought it just as well to have one reporting job that only women could do. In these strictly feminine press conferences, they discussed news and views of special interest to women. Not only did this raise the standing and prestige of newspaperwomen, but editors began to pay more attention to the problems of women citizens. For, naturally, anything the popular First Lady said or did was news.

Before Eleanor Roosevelt entered the White House there were lean days for women reporters in Washington. They had been limited to admiring the president's wife from a distance. About all a reporter could do was describe the clothes she wore at some social function. The press never penetrated the outer fringes of the First Lady's life. She was considered merely a shadow of the president. But Eleanor Roosevelt refused to be a shadowy substance—she emerged as "news" in her own right.

She treated newspaperwomen as honorable human beings, whose good judgment and loyalty she trusted. Only once was her trust ever betrayed—and that reporter was quickly banished from the newspaper world. She answered every conceivable type of question at her press conferences. Breezing in, she would greet them with a cheerful "Good morning, ladies," and shake hands with each reporter, smiling and talking about this and that. She answered their questions good humoredly and frankly—even such questions as: "Is it true that a cockroach was seen in the White House cellar yesterday?" Reporters were interested in whether her new blue hat had dyed her hair blue during the teaming rain on Inauguration Day. They made her decide, on the spot, what the menu would be at a luncheon she was giving the day after tomorrow.

She knew from the beginning what reporters wanted and needed, and she pleased them all—those who liked dignity, and those who liked an occasional surprise announcement or a touch of novelty. She could not give them much front-page news, but she encouraged their questions and answered them all frankly. She believed that the public had a right to know what was going on in the White House. However, she preserved the same "off the record" rule for certain items as did the President.

Unlike former First Ladies, she never turned these meetings with the press over to a secretary. She realized that better personal relations were established if she saw them herself. She made the reporters feel welcome. The life of the First Family was no longer a hushed secret, behind closed doors. She opened the doors—threw away outworn traditions—and let the public in on all their doings.

Now and then she would make a mistake—tell some incident or voice an opinion that might better have been left unsaid. On one such occasion she explained afterwards, "I knew I shouldn't have said that the moment the words were out. It is exactly what I believe, but I should have kept it to myself."

However she knew enough to be discreet, and such slips were infrequent. If she did become too enthusiastic, some vigilant reporter, protecting her from her own words, would interrupt to say: "That's off the record, isn't it?" The First Lady was not supposed to be quoted on anything for which she did not give specific permission. If there was doubt about anything she had said, Eleanor Roosevelt had her secretary read back the conversation from notes.

Once a girl reporter was threatened with exclusion from further conferences by her fellow newspaperwomen, because she had used something presumably said in confidence. Eleanor Roosevelt studied the transcript and decided that the statement in question was not clearly "off the record." She upheld the offending reporter.

At first, as in her newspaper column, Eleanor Roosevelt refused to discuss any political issues with the press. She was afraid that her political opinions might be construed as the opinions of her husband, or of the administration. She even went so far as to say that those asking political questions would be excluded from press conferences. In time, however, she broke all her own rules. Although the general understanding was that she would not discuss politics in any form—her alert mind, ranging from one subject to another, often threw off a thought on political problems. Before long she was answering questions about Supreme Court decisions, bills before Congress, foreign affairs—in fact, everything except political candidates for government positions.

The only taboo which continued to hold at her press conferences was the one on men. It was a bad blow to Washington's spoiled gentlemen of the press, who had been pampered for years. To make matters worse, from their point of view, although they were never allowed to invade the First Lady's conferences, women reporters had an equal status with men at the President's conferences. Eleanor Roosevelt did this purposely. She knew these exclusive interviews would help raise the standards and pay for women reporters.

In self-defense, the newspapermen scoffed and said, condescendingly, that they were glad the girls were having such a good time. One day they were dealt a mortal blow. The "girls" scooped them on a story any one of them would have given his weekly paycheck for: the announcement that beer would be served in the White House. Eleanor Roosevelt had deliberately given this out as a front-page scoop for the ladies of the press.

On the other hand, she never let her reporters scoop each other, and was always careful not to scoop them herself in anything she wrote. She saw to it that they had the information well beforehand. No wonder they called her "Heaven's gift to the press."

CHAMPION OF MINORITIES

Eleanor Roosevelt not only gave women of the press news; she made news for them. They traveled with her everywhere by plane, car, or train. She even telephoned them when she was in an inaccessible spot, so they could get their stories on the wire. They talked with her in taxis and at the swimming pool.

One morning a reporter called and asked if she might see her about a special assignment. Eleanor Roosevelt regretfully said that she just didn't have a minute that day. "I'm due at the hairdresser in half an hour to have my hair set, and right after that I must dress and catch a train to New York. I have a full day tomorrow, too. I wish I could help you, but . . ." Then she had an inspiration. "But there's no good reason why you couldn't meet me at the hairdresser's. I can talk to you while I'm under the dryer."

That morning the First Lady and the reporter shouted questions and answers at each other above the roar of the dryer.

Nearly all newspaperwomen in Washington are Eleanor Roosevelt's devoted admirers. She is so cooperative with reporters most of the time that, when she wants to pay an off-the-record visit to someone, they look the other way.

One reason why ladies of the press worship her is

that she is always thoughtful. One time a reporter was scheduled to accompany her on an early morning plane from New York to Washington. At 7 A.M. the reporter's phone rang. There was a message from Mrs. Roosevelt, saying that all flights from La Guardia had been canceled because of bad weather, and that she was taking the 9:30 train to Washington, car 239, compartment B. She was always conscious of the fact that a reporter was doing a job, and that failure meant disgrace. She often held up a luncheon, to which the press was not admitted, to give them their interview beforehand, thus saving them hours of waiting until the affair was over.

Another time, four newspaperwomen went with her on a rugged trip to Puerto Rico. One of them, convalescing from a serious operation, collapsed from fatigue, and was confined to her hotel room by the doctor. Eleanor Roosevelt didn't know this when she accepted the invitation of the others to come over and swim in their hotel pool. Poised at the edge of the pool—ready to dive in—Eleanor Roosevelt asked, "Where's Ruby?" They told her what had happened. Immediately she said: "Do you think Ruby would like to spend the summer at Campobello?" A summer at Campobello was then four months, and two thousand miles, away, but the invitation still held.

Often there was laughter, mixed with admiration, as the reporters joked about Eleanor Roosevelt's kindness to everyone and everything. Once a group were stranded with her at an airport, while enroute to investigate working conditions for children in a South American community. Eleanor Roosevelt chafed at the delay but finally settled down to a tour of the muddy field that passed for an airport. The only living specimen, beside the owner, was a skinny, sad-looking dog. Eleanor Roosevelt couldn't resist the temptation to inquire about his welfare. "Isn't that just like her," one of the reporters remarked. "She can't investigate conditions for children right now, so the dog has to do." They were much amused.

Nor did her kindness to newspaperwomen protect Eleanor Roosevelt from the satire and merciless fun-making of the reporters. They portrayed her going on trips to Mars and the South Pole; as the newest member of the Supreme Court, sitting on the bench, knitting; or making a speech on some ridiculous topic. Eleanor laughed as much as anyone at their cartoons and anecdotes.

Many cartoons made fun of her activities. One well-known one shows two miners, deep in a mine, looking along the shaft and then at each other. "Why there's Mrs. Roosevelt," one of them exclaims. Her ability to get into inaccessible places was really nothing to joke about. She did visit mines, many times. She always made sure beforehand, however, that the particular mine was not in which the men were superstitious. Some miners, like seamen, believed that a woman "aboard" is bad luck.

Domestic workers benefited directly from her intercession. They were getting very low pay, and housewives were complaining that they couldn't get good servants. Eleanor Roosevelt proposed that a school be organized to train household servants. A number of such W.P.A. schools were started and were highly successful.

Eleanor Roosevelt did not think that barring married women from paid jobs was a good solution to the unemployment problem. "There are three fundamentals for human happiness—love, faith, and work which will produce at least a minimum of material security. These things must be made possible for all human beings—men and women alike.

"Who is to say when a man earns enough to support his family? Who is to know, except the individuals themselves, what they need for daily living, or what their responsibilities are—responsibilities which are often hidden from the public eye? Added to this, who is to say whether a woman needs to work outside her home, for the good of her soul? A fundamental principle of democracy is that while the majority rules, the rights of the minority must also be protected."

Eleanor Roosevelt refused to cross union picket lines, even to attend a Presidential Birthday Ball in Virginia. She discovered that the waitresses at this affair were striking for fifty cents a day increase in pay. She had a deep conviction that waiters, and those with similar jobs, should be paid salaries. At that time, tips were all the pay most of them received.

"They have a right to know what they're going to have in the way of income from week to week, just like anyone else," she said. Eleanor Roosevelt disapproved of tipping, but so long as the system was in force she was a generous tipper. In fact, she was once voted "best tipper" by a union of railway dining car employees. She felt, however, that tipping was unfair, both to customer and worker, and a "lovely excuse" for employers not to pay decent wages.

She tried to be fair on her stand for or against unions, supporting the best in management and the best in labor. She spoke out strongly against dishonest labor leaders, and just as strongly against employers who refused to bargain with employees. She became a member of a union herself, when she started her newspaper column, but never was active in governing it. When some labor issue arose upon which she had a definite opinion or conviction, she spoke out. Otherwise she kept quiet on labor politics. She spoke in favor of the Child Labor Amendment, protective legislation for women, and equal pay for women under the National Recovery Act. Always her interest lay in fair play, for both employee and employer.

One time a group of boys who delivered box lunches to office workers went on strike, complaining that they got no pay from the company. "We have to rely on tips the customers choose to give us. The most we can make is ninety cents a day," one of them explained to the First Lady. "And the average is about twenty-three cents a day. We can't live on that. We want a dollar a day wages. That's what we're striking for."

Her reputation for fair play was so well known that the employer came to her too, with his side of the story. "I can't pay a steady wage," he said. "I make only a nickel profit on each lunch."

At his insistence, Eleanor Roosevelt sat down with all concerned, to talk things over. It was finally decided that the boys would get a minimum of sixty cents a day. Both sides agreed that the quick and easy settlement was entirely due to Eleanor Roosevelt's interest and fairness.

On another occasion, she pleaded for farmers. "If they don't get water to irrigate their land, they're sunk. And if they lose everything they have, it will be important to all of us. We will have to support them." Her realistic approach gained an irrigation project for the farmers in the locality she was visiting.

Every year she makes a speech at a campaign dinner for the Jewish Charitable Organizations. "They do such fine work," she commented, and added: "They must be tired of hearing me by now."

In a day when such things were considered impossible for a wealthy woman, Eleanor Roosevelt was on the board of the Consumers League, wrote in favor of better working and living conditions for laborers, and even marched in a procession of strikers. In spite of her wealth and rigid social background, Eleanor

Roosevelt has always thought on the plane of the little people. They feel her essential goodness, and her concern with the everyday things of their lives. They treat her with a strange mixture of respect and familiarity. They sit next to her on buses and she never snubs them. They say "hello" to her on the street, and she returns their greetings. Everyone of them echoes the sentiment of one who said, "She's a true lady—and she really likes us."

9

A THOUSAND AND ONE PROJECTS

ELEANOR ROOSEVELT has gained an international reputation as a person who is always ready to help a worthy cause. She has helped in many large enterprises, involving the welfare of thousands of people; she has spent even more of her own time helping individuals. Her public projects are well known; her efforts for private citizens are kept very much to herself. But stories of her generosity have leaked out. She has a genuine faith in her fellow man and is always willing to help even a "long shot."

One day a disheveled, unshaven young man walked up to her car in an upstate New York gasoline station. The terrible depression, which President Roosevelt was fighting so vigorously, was now several years old. The young man asked the lady behind the wheel for some money.

Eleanor Roosevelt asked him: "What have you been doing?"

"Looking for a job, like everyone else," he answered. "I tried to get into one of the government work camps. They wouldn't even consider me because I don't have any home address."

Eleanor handed him her card and said: "I'll try to get you into a Civilian Conservation Corps camp. Come to my house at five o'clock Monday afternoon. You can pay me back when you get a job," she added, handing him a ten dollar bill. She drove quickly out of the station, not even waiting for his thanks.

"You'll never see the man or your money again," her friends in the back seat told her. Eleanor just smiled and said: "Perhaps you're right."

Monday afternoon she pulled up to the curb in front of her house at exactly five o'clock. There was no one in sight except a policeman. He walked over and told her he had just chased a man away from her front gate. "He gave me some silly story about an appointment with you at five," he added.

"Where did he go?" Eleanor Roosevelt asked anxiously. Then, seeing the man halfway down the block, she called to him. He walked toward her hesitantly. Eleanor noticed he was scrubbed and freshly

A THOUSAND AND ONE PROJECTS

shaven. She invited him to stay for dinner and later gave him a room for the night.

Eleanor Roosevelt's "tramp" was soon bossing a lumber crew in a CCC Camp. He wrote to her every week. First he returned the money she had lent him, then asked her to start a bank account for him with additional money he would send weekly. Later, when he became foreman and married, his benefactor invited them both to stop for a few days at the White House, on the way home from their honeymoon.

No one knows how many victims of the depression Eleanor Roosevelt personally helped. The number runs into hundreds—perhaps even thousands. When anyone approached her on the street in New York and asked for a nickel for a cup of coffee she gave him her card instead. "Present this to the cook at my home," she said. "She has orders to give you sandwiches and coffee." This one bit of thoughtfulness alone must have warmed many tired hearts, and filled many empty stomachs.

Eleanor Roosevelt took an interest in many things: nursery schools, jobs for unemployed teachers and nurses, and housing projects for a thousand families. One thing she could not do, however, no matter what the job. She could not be a behind-the-desk administrator. She had to dig right into things.

Eleanor Roosevelt could humanize a government project by showing the people that it was not just an intangible organization, with some letters of the alphabet affixed to it. It was, rather, a plan evolved to help people, and the next-door neighbor was a vital part of the plan. One person summed it up for many, when she said: "What Mrs. Roosevelt says is true—WPA workers are people like the rest of us."

Perhaps the largest of Eleanor Roosevelt's public works was the Arthurdale Housing Project. The plan was to build a group of demonstration homes on an eleven-hundred-acre farm, bought by the federal government. Each family was to have several acres of ground on which to raise part of its own food supply. The government was to finance it, with home owners paying it back in small installments, over a twenty-year period.

Eleanor Roosevelt beat a path from Washington to West Virginia. She spent many weeks working out various problems with the people who were going to live at Arthurdale—and there were certainly plenty of problems to be solved! First of all, the ready-built houses didn't fit the foundations which had previously been dug. Then she discovered that heating units for winter occupation had been left out of the plans. These, and other dilemmas, were ironed out by Eleanor Roosevelt's capable hand.

A more intangible problem, and therefore a more difficult one to solve, was the deep-seated distrust these people had for the government, and for each other. Certainly they had little reason to believe in anyone or anything, after a lifetime of being shoved around; but Eleanor Roosevelt worked hard to build up trust and cooperation among them. She helped them organize schools for the children and plant vegetable gardens in their ample acres. Arthurdale took more of Eleanor Roosevelt's money, time, and thought than any other of the hundreds of projects to which she lent a hand.

When the Arthurdale project was accused of being Communistic she replied: "I don't understand why it is considered Communistic to give people a chance to earn their own living and buy their own houses. Any private enterprise could provide the initial capital for other housing projects, just as the government is doing for Arthurdale." In a sense this was a prophecy because it was not long before many industrial companies followed the example set by Arthurdale and launched similar housing projects. Today, Arthurdale is flourishing as a settlement of homes, owned by the people who live in them.

Eleanor Roosevelt made a tour of the Arthurdale homestead after it was completed. She was driven over mountain roads and around hair-pin turns stopping to make eight speeches to outdoor audiences in one day. The people listened eagerly. Most of them realized that here was their one great opportunity to build security and respectability for themselves. They were anxious to make it work. And perhaps even more, they didn't want to let down Eleanor Roosevelt, who had done so much for them.

Another time, while all the rest of Washington was excited over the imminent arrival of the King and Queen of England, the First Lady found time, in the midst of extensive preparations, to worry about a group of sharecroppers. Her informant said they were camped on a highway near Onslow, Missouri, living in three inches of mud. Eleanor sent investigators to look into the situation, this being one of the few times she felt she couldn't go herself.

The investigators reported back a story of misery and suffering. One of them told her, "It was so cold we could only take notes for a few minutes at a time.

A THOUSAND AND ONE PROJECTS

Then we had to stop to warm our hands over a fire. And there are those families, huddled together in huts with little or no heat. It will be even worse for them now—they're being moved off the highways, and will have to keep moving along all the time. I guess the comfortable citizens were offended by the sight of so much misery almost on their doorsteps," he added sarcastically.

Royal celebration or no, this was more than Eleanor could stand. She invited several of the highway sitters to come immediately to the White House. They came: a Negro preacher; a woman with ten children, old and tired at thirty-five; a sad-faced widower with his family piled into an old jalopy.

They sat with Eleanor Roosevelt in the formal Red Room parlor, before the fireplace, and not one felt the least embarrassment. She sat talking over their problems with them until twenty minutes before she was to meet the King and Queen. The First Lady was moved to pity many times but she never showed it. She knew they would resent pity. She merely asked about their problems, letting them tell her a story she already knew, because she realized they wanted to get it off their chests. Then she said, "What can I do for you?"

As soon as she could leave Washington, Eleanor went to Missouri to make her own meticulous investigation. She missed nothing. She was very much moved by the tenderly cared-for flower garden next to a shanty. She admired the courage of the huddled figures with gaunt but clean faces, struggling to live in the miserable, cold huts. She went back to Washington with specific facts to present to the government official who could do something about the situation. And before long something was done.

Because she felt she owed it to the community in which she lived, Eleanor tried particularly hard to improve conditions in Washington, D.C. It shocked and saddened her to see dark, unsanitary slums only a block or two from the Capitol. Surely the city that was the heart of the nation should be especially vigorous in attempts to eliminate these tenements. She took cabinet wives and congressmen's wives with her to see the pitifully crowded homes.

The injection "took." Congress soon passed a bill to eliminate the worst of these alley buildings. And Eleanor Roosevelt was there watching when the first building was torn down. She knew it would take more than this to eliminate the terrible slums of Washington, but at least it was a beginning.

A THOUSAND AND ONE PROJECTS

Public indifference about other situations in Washington disturbed her. "The capital of the nation should set a standard, not merely in the beauty of its buildings and grounds, but in its regard for the welfare of its citizens," she said.

On the outskirts of Washington there was an institution which housed sixty girls, from sixteen to twenty-two years of age, who had been convicted of petty crimes. It operated under the high-sounding name of the National Training School for Girls. The girls lived in dark, unsanitary cells; there was one bathroom to twenty-five girls. It was called a school, but there were no teachers, no psychiatrist, and only a part-time doctor.

Its buildings were situated in the midst of beautiful, wooded hills, but since there were not enough guards for adequate supervision out-of-doors, the girls were never allowed out. They even went through underground passageways when passing from one building to another. The blue skies and green meadows and tall trees were there, but they offered these girls no escape from the dull routine of their days.

Eleanor Roosevelt decided something had to be done. She started the ball rolling by having a garden party on the White House lawn, to which she invited all sixty of the girls. It created quite a stir in Washington circles, but as usual, Eleanor went ahead, doing what she thought she should. In fact, on this occasion she probably was pleased with the comments on her action, because it focused interest on the project. Such interest—approving or disapproving—would pave the way for the practical appeal she wished to make to the public mind. She had her say about the National Training School at a public meeting where the subject just "happened" to come up—dragged in, no doubt, by Eleanor, who never let pass an opportunity to plug a reform dear to her heart. She said, "As things stand now, these girls will always be a burden to the taxpayers. When they get out of this 'school,' they'll only go on to prisons, insane asylums, and public hospitals. The cost of their care will be continuously greater for all of you."

Her logic turned the trick where a more sentimental appeal would have failed. The next session of Congress voted to allot $100,000 to the school. A model kitchen was built to teach the girls cooking, a vocational school was organized in which they could learn beauticians' jobs, clerical work, and salesmanship. The living quarters were made clean and adequate. When these alterations were completed, the girls sent a special invitation to Eleanor Roosevelt to have lunch with them in their new dining room. They wanted to thank her for their new lives.

Not only the young people, but the old folks as well benefited by her interest. A Negro friend wrote of having visited a home for the aged, where a patient had not been turned over in his bed for six weeks. Eleanor went and found cots crowded together in one room. There were but one registered nurse and fourteen unskilled helpers to take care of 130 bedridden people. She learned that only sixty-three cents a day was spent on food for each of the seven hundred inmates. She spread the word around where it would do the most good. Congress started an investigation and invited Eleanor to appear before them to tell of the conditions she had seen. This was the first time a First Lady had been summoned before Congress.

She stood there, her expressive hands occasionally emphasizing how strongly she felt what she was saying. "We should be ashamed." Her words came forcefully. "I was sickened. If that is the way we care for people who are not able to care for themselves, we are at a pretty low ebb of civilization." And once again, Congress, persuaded by her simple eloquence, appropriated the funds to remedy the disgraceful situation.

The list of her projects is varied and endless. She started a campaign to have the Social Security Act include domestic servants. She was active in a national health program to make medical aid available to low-income groups.

One of her lesser-known interests was a long battle for electricity in rural areas. She found that the farmers themselves were often the chief opponents of progress. She allied herself with the women on these farms who had "so little chance for anything but work and the bare necessities of life, in return for the whole family's drudgery." She told these farmers frankly, "I have no sympathy with the farmer who can see the benefit of electricity in his barn but not in his home."

Eleanor Roosevelt's ceaseless efforts to help people has not been confined only to her own country. During the war she "adopted" many children. She supported a war orphan in China, a twelve-year-old boy in Spain, a fifteen-year-old Polish girl refugee. Realizing that these children could not be safely brought to this country because of submarines and mines, she dug deeply into her pocketbook for money to keep them fed and clothed as near their own homes as possible. Eleanor worked hard to gain help for civil-

A THOUSAND AND ONE PROJECTS

ians in war-torn countries and was always at the head of any list of contributors. She made many speeches on behalf of the needy and suffering, urging Americans not to forget the universal code of all decent people: "Love thy neighbor."

Eleanor Roosevelt continually worked to bring the people and the government closer together. It bothered her, occasionally, that she couldn't see more immediate results in her work. Sometimes results took a long time to materialize. Then she would sigh and say that she was sure "government was designed to teach patience." She had plenty of that.

10

YOUNG PEOPLE

THE First Lady greeted the group of young men and women from the First Church of Albein, Ohio, with a smile and handclasp for each. She led them into her study. They seemed to her just like any other young people: a little sadder, perhaps, than some she had worked with, but otherwise no different. Yet she knew that she was face to face with a cross section of the so-called "lost generation"—a group of young people made desolate by a terrible depression, a catastrophe that denied them jobs, hope, or a future. For this was 1932, at the height of the greatest depression the world has ever known.

One of the boys spoke first: "What can I do, Mrs. Roosevelt? I'm seventeen and just out of high school. I thought since I couldn't get a job I'd go back to school for another year, but the schools are overcrowded, they don't want us there."

YOUNG PEOPLE

A tired-faced girl said, "I'm sick of being a burden to my family. My father has no job and there isn't enough money even to take care of the younger children. I'm eighteen; how can I expect to go on living at home if I can't get a job and contribute something?"

A young couple looked at each other and then at Mrs. Roosevelt. He said, "We want to get married, but how can we, with no home and no hope of a job for either of us?"

"Yes!" added a tall, serious boy from a far corner of the room, "What good does it do us to live in a democracy? Maybe we'd be better off under a socialistic or communistic government—at least then we could work."

Eleanor Roosevelt listened in silent sympathy and understanding. She didn't blame them at all for their bitterness. Their government had failed them! She talked quietly with them for hours, promising to do everything in her power to help. After having lunch with her, they left the White House. They went back to Ohio, knowing that an influential friend would be working hard for them.

It was a long, difficult task to get opportunities, jobs, education, and training for a million stranded young people. Eleanor found it difficult to convince adults that the problem of young people was a serious one, perhaps the most serious of all. With so many heads of families out of work, nearly all the attention was focused on their difficulties. But every time she talked with a government official or relief administrator, Eleanor Roosevelt managed, somehow, to drag into the conversation some discussion of the young folks' pressing problems. "Some of the relief funds must be used to help them," she urged.

One of her best job-creating ideas was that of internships in public service. Two young people—John and Helen—are typical of the many who, with the help of this plan, made their way through a depression-ridden world.

John was assigned as an assistant in the health department of a large city. He didn't supplant any other person, he was just added to the staff as an apprentice. His salary was paid out of relief funds. Being industrious, he learned the work of his department very thoroughly. A few years later, one of the older men in the department died, and John was promoted to his position. A manufactured opportunity, plus his own hard work, resulted in permanent security for

YOUNG PEOPLE

John. It gave him a new, stronger belief in his government.

Under a similar plan, Helen went to work in a welfare agency in her own community. She became engrossed in the problems of misplaced and homeless children. After several years of practical experience, she managed, through self-sacrifice and hard work, to save enough money to go back to school and complete her education for a career in professional social work. She later became head of the organization in which she had been an apprentice.

Eleanor Roosevelt's apprenticeship plan was an effort to find an answer to the complaint she heard so many times: "I can't get a job because I have no experience, and how can I get experience if I can't get a job?" She knew, of course, that for every youngster the government helped, there were seven it could not reach. But even one in eight was much better than nothing.

Many years before there was any depression, Eleanor Roosevelt had been interested in young people. Nothing could keep her away from a meeting which benefited a youth organization. One time a large luncheon was held in New York to raise camp funds for underprivileged children. It was a big social event with lots of fuss and feathers. All New York society had been invited to attend. Eleanor Roosevelt was to be the principal guest speaker.

On the morning of the day set for the luncheon, the front page of the New York *Times* carried two stories. A bomb had been intercepted in Governor Franklin D. Roosevelt's mail that morning in Albany. The second item stated that Anna Roosevelt's house had been burned to the ground the night before, while she and her husband were honeymooning in Europe.

The chairman of the luncheon wrung her hands in despair, and almost wept on the shoulder of the co-chairman. The whole affair would be a fiasco. The principal guest would surely never show up now! But right on the dot, Eleanor arrived. The chairman greeted her warmly. "I never expected to see you after I read the morning paper," she said. Eleanor answered matter-of-factly, "I called Albany and everything was fine. As for Anna's house, it's gone and there's nothing anyone can do." And the luncheon proceeded as scheduled.

Not all of her work with youth organizations was successful. She had her disappointments too. Eleanor

Roosevelt's patronage of the American Youth Congress brought added criticism down on her unprotected head. Fortunately though, just as many people praised her courage in advising the group and her refusal to be intimidated. Most people felt that whether the A.Y.C. had communism in its ranks or not, Eleanor deserved a great deal of credit for the friendly counseling and constructive guidance she tried to give these young people.

As a matter of fact, Eleanor Roosevelt was the only real help these young people could find outside the radical movement. Left to themselves, many more would have turned readily to communism. Eleanor's guidance redirected many young minds into democratic channels. She tried to justify the attitude of these young unemployed men and women: "We have not made democracy work so they can find their place in it," she said. "Why should they feel a responsibility for defending it until we prove it is worth defending?"

She was always impressed with the earnestness of this group of young people. She never quite believed that they were a group of Communists. "They open and close the meeting with a prayer—so they are not irreligious. And although I met a few at their meetings who had a socialistic philosophy, these few did not represent a controlling force by any means. We think so much of communism, which holds such a small place in their ranks, that we let it cover up the really important problems of these young people." Then she added: "Even if the group is infiltrated with Communists, that is no reason for turning our backs on all the others. We should find out the facts and help them."

But the A.Y.C. did not keep faith with Eleanor. When it came to a showdown, they shamed her before her guests. The group met at the White House. When guests there complained about this open championship of a group known to have Communists in their ranks, Eleanor Roosevelt said: "I believe in the young people. To show you their good faith, I'll just ask the Communists in the group to rise and identify themselves. There are only a few anyway and this will show you that everything is above board."

She stood before the group and made her simple request. Her words sounded clearly the length of the room. But no one stood up. There was a moment of tense silence, then the First Lady turned and walked quickly from the room. Pain and disillusionment showed in her face.

YOUNG PEOPLE

Although such an experience could not shake her basic faith in young people, it made her more wary of sponsoring any group. She grew increasingly suspicious of radical groups, but she still maintained that young people should have a chance to express their views. She had faith in them, but she knew they could persist longer in a mistaken belief than any other group of people. "I wish I were young so that I didn't have to consider so many sides of every subject," she said once. "It is so much easier to be enthusiastic than to reason."

Eleanor Roosevelt listened to questions and invited many troubled young people to the White House for private talks. One boy said: "She is the First Lady of America not because she is the President's wife, but because of her courage and work for America, her tolerance and understanding."

Her sense of fairness extended to all things, even to public criticism of her children when they deserved it. When one of her sons remarked that some of the delegates to the American Youth Congress had not shown very good manners, she turned on him: "Who are you to talk about bad manners? You never had to fight for an education, or search for a job, or delay your marriage for lack of money."

Eleanor became interested in the International Student Service Group. She lent them her cottage at Campobello for their meetings, during two summers. This organization was originally designed to give financial aid to foreign students studying in the United States. When war broke out in Europe, their object became the developing of a feeling of world responsibility among students to combat the isolationist point of view.

She traveled around from campus to campus, explaining democracy to college students. After her lecture she would always talk informally with students in the dean's office. More than one woman's college extended her an invitation to be its president. But she didn't want any such limitations.

One of her chief interests today still is the Wiltwick School for Delinquent Children. She helps raise funds for this very fine institution. She gives her verbal and written support to its progressive methods and therapeutic work. And she has picnics at her cottage for the children.

But Eleanor Roosevelt did more than help organizations of young people. Her interests in them as individuals began with interest in her children and their friends. This gradually evolved into a deep-

YOUNG PEOPLE

seated liking for all young people and a real desire to be with them and talk with them, to keep in close touch their ideas and dreams.

Although she was only honorary president—a title conferred on every First Lady—of the Girl Scouts and Campfire Girls, she seemed to find more time for them in her busy schedule than most honorary officers.

Her willingness to help them dated almost from her first day in the White House. The Girl Scouts' twenty-first anniversary occurred about a week after Mrs. Roosevelt moved into the White House. Everyone thought it impossible to get any of her time on such short notice. It would be her first public appearance since coming to Washington. It looked hopeless, but they asked anyway. She glanced at her calendar. "I have one hour free, from two to three, that afternoon," she said, "if you can use it."

The whole program was changed, streets were blocked off, and the police force was called out in full to escort her to the place where she was going to speak. Eleanor laughed at all this falderal and put a stop to it then and there for all future occasions.

One Christmas a specially picked group of Scouts was going to stand on the lawn of the White House and serenade the First Lady. It was very cold so they were cautioned to dress warmly. "Wear your red flannels, heavy sweaters, and coats. If you haven't anything else, wear your wool bathing suits under your other clothing," they were told. "You'll be all in red capes and hoods and no one will know what you have on underneath."

Eleanor took one look at the group of little girls singing in the cold winter night, and invited them into the East Room. After one carol outside, with lanterns gleaming for the benefit of the news photographers, the Scouts shed their red capes at the door and went into the warm room. Unfortunately there was no opportunity to shed wool bathing suits and flannels. Many a small Scout squirmed and wriggled and scratched.

A few minutes later they forgot their troubles. The First Lady, in a sheer icicle blue gown, with a white shawl over her shoulders and a welcoming smile on her face, came toward them. None of them had ever seen her before—only horrible pictures of her in newspapers, and comments from their elders about how homely she was. They gasped, "Why, she's beautiful."

She made them feel she was hostess to honored guests. As they left she shook each hand graciously and said earnestly, "I can't tell you how much I've enjoyed it." The little girls floated out of the White House and walked on clouds all the way home.

During a campaign to promote safety measures in the home, she gave another group of Scouts permission to inspect the White House for hazards. They checked attic pipes for asbestos covering, and bottles in the medicine chest cabinets for poison plainly marked on them; then tested gas cocks in the kitchen, and looked for gripping mats under the rugs. The White House stood the test quite well.

Eleanor Roosevelt, not caring how it might make her look or what embarrassment it might cause her, let them report their findings over the air without any preliminaries. "I'm at your mercy," she said as they started firing questions at her.

When a Western Hemisphere Conference of Girl Scouts and Girl Guides was held in Westchester County, New York, Eleanor Roosevelt was invited to speak to the group. Scouts from fifteen countries and twenty-six of the United States were to be there. She said that of course she'd be glad to come.

She arrived without fanfare and, after shaking hands with 240 girls and counselors, had lunch with them in their mess hall. After lunch she stood up and spoke briefly to the representatives of Latin and South American countries, Canada, and the United States. "Let us each love our country, but look at it with understanding and clear-sighted eyes—for only thus can you young people hope to bring to our West Hemisphere a better future and to make this hemisphere a better neighbor for the rest of the world."

In the early afternoon there was a very colorful flag ceremony with the flags of all the fifteen countries passing in review before their honored guest. She stood at attention, stirred by the roll of drums and sound of their voices in patriotic song.

Later, Eleanor Roosevelt walked around the camp. She stopped to watch one group do an American square dance, to watch another group do an Argentine folk dance. The girls swapped stories with her and each other. They exchanged recipes for shrimps with cocoanut milk, Canadian goulash, and chicken Muquecal. The First Lady was very much interested. She talked for long hours with the girls. One scout said, "She's swell! She doesn't talk down to us. She treats us as equals—not as little girls!"

Although she thought their organizations for young people were fine, Eleanor Roosevelt disliked any regimentation of young people. Ten years before a program of military training became a fact, Eleanor Roosevelt was talking to the President about it. "I dislike the idea very much," she said. "It smacks too much of regimentation. I think the best thing is universal 'citizenship service' ": training in government mechanical skills, agriculture, and perhaps some military skills. The war solved that problem for a time, and we had conscription because it was necessary.

Today, Eleanor Roosevelt says: "I realize that until the United Nations has set up a permanent police force which can be used against aggressors anywhere, we must keep our country sufficiently strong to defend ourselves. This may mean universal military training. But I hope that in time it will be training for citizenship, with the education and future plans of these young people taken into consideration in the type of work assigned."

She thinks that the responsibilities of young people in a democracy are very simple. "They should prepare themselves to be useful citizens by using their educational opportunities to the best advantage, by developing all of their capacities, and by contributing to the life of the community in which they live," she says. "We would have a finer, stronger nation if young people gave as much of themselves to their country in time of peace as they do in time of war."

11

THE LADY OF WASHINGTON SQUARE

ELEANOR ROOSEVELT now lives in an apartment on Washington Square in New York. This is her permanent address, but she is there very little of the time. Her base of operations is a triangular area with one apex at Hyde Park, another at Lake Success, and the third in New York. And, of course, she makes many trips away from home base, to California, Paris, or London.

Her modern apartment in New York is a homey place. Family portraits, ship models, and other treasures crowd her living room. Books of all kinds fill the bookshelves, and a few special favorites stand between book ends on the table. Very few books in this large library are first editions; no volume was chosen for its fine binding. It is a well-read collection, reflecting the tastes of a person interested in just about everything.

The lady of the house has the same lack of formality as her apartment. Her ideas are modern, yet she remains simple and somewhat old-fashioned, in the best sense of the word. She likes these living quarters, she says, because she can get a glimpse of the Hudson River from her window.

When Eleanor Roosevelt craves a little peace and quiet, she drives up to Hyde Park, with the intention of resting there for a few days. But she rarely has time to hang up her hat before some job calls her back again. So, breathing one last lungful of fresh country air, she heads for New York again. She likes Manhattan, though. "I enjoy the hurry and bustle, the mixture of people, and the great variety of things they are doing. It stimulates me to get out and do something." As if she needed such stimulation!

Every morning she sits at the desk in the Washington Square apartment, dictating her daily column to her secretary and answering her multitudinous mail. Despite frequent interruptions by the telephone, she doesn't take long to get this work done. The words flow easily from her lips; she hesitates only now and then, for emphasis.

Eleanor Roosevelt has certainly upset the tradition that presidents' widows should be seldom seen and never heard. After President Roosevelt's death, she announced that she intended to lead a "private and inconspicuous existence." She hasn't yet had time to get around to it. She still puts in the bustling kind of day a woman thirty years younger would find exhausting. She is more active now than she ever was as First Lady.

Certainly today, as a representative to the United Nations, she is more of a public figure than when Franklin Roosevelt was alive. When the United Nations was first being formed, our State Department was very anxious to have a woman on the team. She seemed the ideal choice. Everyone was happy when President Truman gave Eleanor Roosevelt the appointment. She took the job gladly, and dedicated herself to the United Nations and the cause of peace with the same wisdom and determination she shows in everything she does.

"I consider it an honor to work with the United Nations," she said, when she accepted the appointment. "I hope I can deserve the confidence of those who appointed me and the good will and respect of those who work with me."

The new appointee got along fine with the State Department, until that body did a reverse end run on the Palestine question. That offended Eleanor's sense of fairness, and her criticism became quite sharp. She did not hesitate to speak her mind on what she didn't like about this country's foreign policy.

The State Department has had a rather rude awakening. Eleanor Roosevelt does not always behave like the idealistic but impractical woman they expected her to be. There are times when she even gets "real tough" about an issue and speaks out at a United Nations meeting, and at other times she changes many "nos" to "yeses," or "maybes," by her sensible, humble suggestions.

When she first began work with the United Nations, Eleanor Roosevelt had had little experience in dealing with public affairs at the diplomatic level. She was first to admit that her knowledge was limited. But she started with a strong desire to learn and understand, and with a real feeling of good will for all people.

With her appointment to the Human Rights Commission of the United Nations, she began a new chapter in her wide expanse of activities. She sits with the social, humanitarian, and cultural committees dealing with such world problems as refugees, world health, and equality of women. These are, in new garb, the same principles she has been fighting for on the home front for years.

The other members of the commission elected her to be their chairman. They didn't realize what an unorthodox chairman she would be. Why, she actually read the texts of what had gone on in previous meetings, word for word, instead of just skimming. And she remarked, while in Geneva for a United Nations meeting, that her hotel accommodations "seemed unnecessarily elegant." She even attended every session she was supposed to attend. When she was invited to a luncheon by the King and Queen of England, she replied: "I'd be delighted to come, but I'll have to leave early to attend a subcommittee meeting.

Her chairmanship of the Human Rights Commission is dispatched with the same efficiency with which she runs her private life. One year the commission convened in early December. The delegates groaned. "That means none of us will get home for Christmas. You know how these conferences drag on and on," they said. But they reckoned without their chairman. She has seventeen grandchildren, and feels very strongly about spending Christmas with her family.

On December 3 she announced: "I expect delegates

to attend to all matters on the agenda within two weeks." On December 17, the commission wound up its last piece of business. Eleanor Roosevelt's comment on this modern miracle was simply: "I just made them work from the beginning, the way delegates usually work the last few days of a conference."

Some time later, Eleanor Roosevelt presided at a meeting which climaxed her first three years of work in the United Nations. The Commission of Human Rights, after more than one hundred meetings, had finally ratified the preamble and twenty-eight articles of a document known as the Universal Declaration of Human Rights. This charter set standards for the fifty-eight member nations in regard to such rights as freedom from arbitrary arrest, the right of the individual to have an education, and the right of every person to work for a living. These are the privileges that we take for granted in the United States, but they do not exist in many other countries.

It was a long hard struggle to get fifty-eight different races, nationalities, and governments to agree to these principles, but they finally did. Once passed by the Economic and Social Council, the Declaration would have the weight of a treaty, and every nation ratifying it would agree to make its laws conform to these principles. The next step will be to devise a means of enforcing the Declaration, and of providing specific penalties for nations violating it.

Eleanor Roosevelt knows that it is not just foolish optimism to hope that, in the future, all nations may be brought together in peaceful, lasting unity. The first great step—the ratification of the Declaration—has been taken and, as she says: "These articles will be the cornerstone in the building of a peaceful world."

At meetings of the United Nations she expresses her beliefs frankly and forcibly. She has a broad, tolerant viewpoint. Even her adversaries call her one of the greatest women in America. Her fellow delegates admire her keen grasp of world affairs. When she enters the assembly, all other representatives spontaneously rise to their feet. They accord this honor only to her.

It is more than her honesty and straightforward ability that earns Eleanor Roosevelt such homage. In a world where nearly everyone has some ax to grind, she is a noble exception. She is a tower of unselfishness in an organization where individuals and nations are looking out primarily for their own interests. To many, she is the American conscience—what we might all do in the interest of world peace if we had the ability, opportunity, and the necessary "push."

Eleanor seldom allows herself the luxury of losing her patience. But she has temporarily misplaced it several times at United Nations meetings, when some politician has held forth on the perfection of our country, and the lowliness of all others. She said on one such occasion: "We cannot always be sure our government is right. We shall do our best to make it so, but we cannot believe in the rightness of some things that we know exist here. We know human nature is not perfect—in the United States as well as elsewhere. I would like to feel sure that some way was found to watch us as well as other nations."

Nothing could show more clearly that she is a thoughtful, truth-seeking person—not a blind patriot.

Eleanor Roosevelt is the kind of person who will continue to grow as long as she lives; she can't stand still; she must keep developing. Her enthusiasm is as strong as ever. At United Nations meetings, as she listens to a speech by another delegate, her enthusiasm often gets the better of her, and she grasps the triangular sign in front of her and waves it frantically, as a signal that she wants to say something.

She is now more at ease as a speaker than when she first faced an audience years ago. She also feels more free to speak, knowing that her ideas will be credited only to her, not to the President or the Administration.

Although she has been called everything, from a pacifist to a warmonger, her views on world peace are very simple. It is just a matter of cooperation, she believes, and an ability to see the other fellow's point of view. World peace must be built upon confidence in one another. To those who accuse her of being too idealistic, she answers: "Remember that every step forward is the product of someone who dreamed dreams."

She is not dogmatic; she wishes only that the nations will do something to promote world peace—not necessarily in her way.

She ended one speech about peace for the future by saying, "Let's do something. If we don't do what I have suggested, let's do something else—but for heaven's sake, let's do something." Then she added: "The United States could assume leadership in the United Nations if we only knew what we wanted and felt strongly about it."

Someone once asked her what she thought of the

Russian delegates with whom she came in contact at the United Nations meetings. She answered, "As individuals, I like them very much. As representatives of their government, I find them at times irritating, and at times difficult to work with. They are tied by instructions given them by their government and are allowed very little, if any, individual flexibility, which makes compromise and cooperation very difficult."

Not even the importance of being an official delegate to the United Nations can keep Eleanor Roosevelt from being herself. She puts in the same hard day of work she always has. Only an exceptionally well-disciplined person could carry out her program. When her United Nations committees are in session, she is there at nine in the morning and often doesn't get home until seven-thirty at night. When, for the thousandth time, someone marveled at all she accomplishes, she merely said, "I manage to do a lot because I'm interested in my work, and because I am blessed with good health and don't worry about things that have already happened."

Representing the United States at the United Nations is only the first of Eleanor's many post-White House activities. She has still a colossal daily schedule of talk, conferences, and personal appearances. She frequently lectures on such favorite topics of her own as international government, education, Negro problems, and labor unions for domestic workers.

Time is so precious to her that she has learned to make the most of spare moments of rest. She can fall asleep at will and has perfected the art of taking brief naps at public gatherings. Her cat-nap technique is so accomplished that only those within a few feet of her can tell she's asleep.

She can still manage a day in which she attends a breakfast conference at Bryn Mawr College, in Pennsylvania, speaks at a fund-raising luncheon for a boys' school in New York, drives to Poughkeepsie for a Girl Scout powwow in the evening—and keeps her daily column, monthly magazine page, and multitudinous correspondence up to date.

Someone once asked her what she looked forward to most in her life out of the White House. She answered simply: "Freedom from public notice." But she will never have it, she just can't keep out of things. Her enthusiasm for a good cause is as great today as it ever was.

There seems little chance that Eleanor Roosevelt's frequently expressed desire "to spend the rest of my days in the country" will be fulfilled. Her present program of activities would certainly not allow for that. One woman, when she heard her express this wish, said with scorn, "Oh, you mean one of those fancy city houses in the country—not a real country home."

Eleanor answered in her usual practical manner: "If you mean I'd like electricity, hot water, and a few other conveniences, I guess you're right. I can't see, though, that it detracts from the beauty of country living to have a few conveniences which take the drudgery out of it." She doesn't seem, however, destined to settle down in any one place for very long— country or city.

So much of her life has been spent in the spotlight, that she might well be glad to rest in oblivion for the remainder of her days. But she is too much of a personality; people are too interested in everything she does. When she wasn't seen in her usual haunts for two days, rumors started flying: that she had a nervous breakdown, that she was dying of cancer, that she was about to marry again.

When this gossip reached her ears Eleanor chuckled. "Though I realize my age might give rise to the first two surmises," she said, "it should certainly preclude the last."

Eleanor is very happy in her United Nations work and considers it the climax of her career, but she could have had a dozen other posts, such as Senator from New York, or cabinet member, or high office in any one of several government agencies. She has always said she was not interested in holding public office, probably because she thinks her freedom would be limited in the multitude of tasks she feels should be done. Pressed for an exact reason she once said: "I certainly could not run for political office while my husband was so active in politics. I am too old now. I think this is a time when young people should be encouraged to go into politics—not old ladies."

She has been an ardent feminist and a strong champion for woman's rights, but she has consistently refused all offers of high public office for herself. When asked if she felt it would have been nice to have been born a man, she answered, "No. I've often wished to be more effective as a woman—but I never felt that trousers could do the trick."

People who know her only through newspapers and magazines think of her as a homely woman, but those who have met her face to face say that pictures fail to show the queenliness and kindliness which give her face real beauty. She is not homely—merely unphotogenic. She herself has said, "One has to be philosophical about pictures."

Eleanor claims that her appearance was somewhat improved by the acquisition of "two lovely new porcelain teeth." These replaced the two front teeth she had knocked out in an auto accident. It is like her to have felt so badly about falling asleep at the wheel that she penalized herself beyond the temporary suspension of her license. She confined her driving, for a long time, to the immediate vicinity of Hyde Park, though this must frequently have been very inconvenient.

When one considers how much praise and admiration have been heaped upon her, her modesty is unbelievable. She couldn't understand why, when she went abroad by plane during the war, such elaborate precautions were taken for her safety. What a target for the Luftwaffe she would have been! She remarked that the aircraft crew seemed surprised to have a woman aboard. Evidently it never occurred to her that their surprise might have something to do with who that woman was.

THE LADY OF WASHINGTON SQUARE

She remarked to a friend that she must be getting old, when a young lady, riding with her in a bus, had risen and offered Eleanor her seat. Again it never occurred to her that this courtesy was a personal tribute.

She wishes always to do as much for herself as possible and be the least possible trouble to others. One morning at Hyde Park, she awoke to discover that nearly two feet of snow had fallen during the night. She was scheduled to broadcast that morning from Poughkeepsie, five miles away. Only main roads, at best, would be plowed by then, and it looked as though the broadcast would have to be canceled.

The telephone rang in Eleanor's study. It was the studio executive. "I really don't know what to do. I can send a sleigh to pick you up at the main road but I doubt that a horse could get through the road leading into your place," he said. "Don't worry," she answered, "I'll get to the highway all right."

An hour before broadcast time she set out. She plowed her way through, on foot, for two miles. Sometimes she had to make her way through shoulder-high drifts, piled up at the sides of the road by the wind, but she reached the highway. After the broadcast she was driven back to her jumping-off place, and she calmly hiked the two miles back to her home. "It was easy returning," she said, "because I could step in the tracks I had made on the way out."

When she went to Geneva to attend a meeting of the United Nations Commission on Human Rights, she was received with great ceremony and honor. The Swiss people waited eagerly for a glimpse of her, although one might think that, accustomed as they were to foreign dignitaries, they'd have been very bored with important people by then. Eleanor Roosevelt, however, was more to them than a statesman, more than the head of a government—she was unique. They crowded around the hotel where the meeting was to be held.

European heads of government urged her to visit them and talk to their people during her United Nations trips. "It would do more for morale than anything we can think of," kings, queens, and presidents would say. Even Stalin was no exception. His first words of greeting to Elliott Roosevelt, on his visit to Russia, were, "When is your mother coming?"

When she visited London to unveil a statue of her late husband, a London newspaper said: "She is a welcome not only for her great name, but for her own endearing qualities of heart and mind." Winston Churchill added, "We must ascribe to her the marvelous feat that a crippled man, victim of a cruel affliction, was able for more than ten years to ride the storms of peace and war at the helm of the United States. The debt we owe to President Roosevelt we also owe to her."

As she entered her London hotel, all the men in the crowd outside respectfully removed their hats. That evening, as she entered the royal box at Covent Garden, the hall shook with a thundering ovation.

The position she holds in the world today far surpasses that which she held when she was First Lady, although it is unofficial. A recent poll conducted by the *Woman's Home Companion* indicates that in the minds of thousands of readers she is the most popular living American of either sex. The New York *Times* once said:

"She could be elected 'Mrs. America' by a landslide of votes." There are a great many who would elect her "First Lady of the World."

As long as she lives, Eleanor Roosevelt will have a hand in shaping her country's destinies—and the destinies of the world.

ACKNOWLEDGMENTS

I AM GRATEFUL indeed to the many friends of Mrs. Roosevelt who gave so generously of their time in personal interviews to answer questions put by a sometimes-persistent author. They supplied many of the incidents that are recounted in this inspiring story.

I also want to thank those in charge of the newspaper and periodical rooms of the New York Public Library and the Brooklyn Public Library who helped me dig out the hundreds of items in their files that related to my subject, as well as the complete sequence of *My Day*.

I checked some of my facts and anecdotes by referring to *This Is My Story* by Eleanor Roosevelt, published by Harper & Brothers; and *Eleanor Roosevelt* by Ruby Black.

Most of all I want to thank Eleanor Roosevelt for her kindness in permitting me to write this book for girls; for her cooperation once I had started it; and for her patience in checking it after it was written.

INDEX

Allenswood, 34-35, 38, 40, 41
American Youth Congress, 155-57
Arthurdale Housing Project, 140-42

Campobello Island, 70, 130, 158
Children, Eleanor Roosevelt's (*see also* Anna, Elliott, Franklin Jr., James), 62, 69-71, 82, 83, 84, 90, 109, 116
Consumers League, 45, 65, 135

D.A.R., 123

Education, Eleanor Roosevelt's, 12-13, 23-24, 34-41
Energy, Eleanor Roosevelt's, 61, 81, 84, 96, 98, 104, 112-14, 166, 174-76, 179

Farmers, 28, 95, 119, 135, 142-44, 148

Girl Scouts, 159-61, 175
Grandchildren, Eleanor Roosevelt's, 83, 97, 169

Hall, Eddie (uncle), 18, 26, 43
Hall, Grandfather, 4, 5, 25
Hall, Grandmother, 18, 19, 21, 22, 23, 28, 29, 30, 31, 32, 33, 35, 38, 39, 40, 41, 43, 44, 47, 50, 53
Hall, Maude (aunt), 18, 26, 29, 31, 38, 43, 55
Hall, Pussie (aunt), 18, 25, 26, 29, 31, 38, 43, 55
Hall, Vallie (uncle), 18, 19, 20, 26, 42
Human Rights Commission; *see* United Nations
Hyde Park, 27, 48, 54, 165, 166, 178, 179

King and Queen of England, 92, 93-94, 142, 143, 169

Labor, 94, 119, 133-35, 175

INDEX

Minorities; *see* Farmers, Negroes, Women, Youth
Music, 23, 25-26, 39, 93, 98
My Day, 106-109, 111

Negro, Negroes, 112, 119, 120-23, 124, 143, 147, 175
Newspaperwomen, 83, 97, 113, 119, 124-25, 127-31

Pegler, Westbrook, 107-109, 117
Pets, 6, 27, 28, 70-71, 131
Philanthropies, 19, 101-102, 104, 105, 106, 109, 110, 115, 117, 137-49, 158
Public office, 79-80, 177

Roosevelt, Anna Eleanor (daughter), 57, 71-72, 154
Roosevelt, Anna Hall (mother), 2, 3, 4-5, 6, 9, 12, 13-16
Roosevelt, Elliott (son), 60, 180
Roosevelt, Elliott Jr. (brother), 8, 9, 13, 18
Roosevelt, Elliott Sr. (father), 1-3, 5-11, 12, 13, 16, 17, 19, 20, 21, 27
Roosevelt, Franklin D., 30, 44-45, 47-51, 53-55, 56, 60, 61, 62, 66-68, 69, 73, 74, 75, 76, 77, 78, 79, 80, 82, 83, 84, 87, 89, 90, 99, 115, 126, 128, 137, 154, 167, 180, 181
Roosevelt, Franklin Jr. (son), 61, 70
Roosevelt, Hall (brother), 12, 13, 18, 28, 43
Roosevelt, James (son), 58, 115, 116
Roosevelt, Mrs., Sr. (Sara Delano) (mother-in-law), 56-57, 58, 59, 64, 66-67, 99
Roosevelt, Theodore (uncle), 5, 29, 30, 50, 52, 53, 56

Shyness and fears, childhood, 6-8, 9, 12, 14, 15, 27, 29, 30, 31, 44, 45, 49, 54, 58-59, 66, 69
Social consciousness, early, 10-11, 18, 19, 20, 45
Souvestre, Mlle., 35, 36-37, 38, 39-40, 41
Sports, 30, 38-39, 58-59, 69, 70, 96

Teetotalism, 11, 78, 128
Thompson, Malvina, 110
Tivoli, 24, 26, 28
Todhunter School, 68-69

United Nations, 163, 167-74, 177, 180
  Human Rights Commission, 168-71, 180

Washington Square, 165, 166
White House, 77, 78, 81, 85, 88-93, 95-96, 97, 100, 105, 106, 123, 125, 126, 128, 139, 143, 146, 151, 156, 157, 159, 161
Women (*see also* Newspaperwomen), 60, 65, 75, 111, 114, 115, 119, 124, 132, 134, 148, 168, 177

[184]

INDEX

League of Women Voters, 64
Women's Division, Democratic State Committee, 64
Women's Trade Union League, 65
World War I activities, 62-63

World War II activities, 83-87, 148-49

Youth, activities with, 68-69, 119, 145-47, 150-64, 175

CPSIA information can be obtained
at www.ICGtesting.com
Printed in the USA
LVHW101224291120
672944LV00013B/660